W9-BDE-881

3-Minute Motivators

More than 200 simple ways to reach, teach, and achieve more than you ever imagined

Kathy Paterson

Revised and Expanded Edition

Pembroke Publishers Limited

© 2014 Pembroke Publishers
538 Hood Road
Markham, Ontario, Canada L3R 3K9
www.pembrokepublishers.com

Distributed in the U.S. by Stenhouse Publishers
480 Congress Street
Portland, ME 04101
www.stenhouse.com

All rights reserved.
No part of this publication may be reproduced in any form or by any means electronic
or mechanical, including photocopy, scanning, recording, or any information, storage
or retrieval system, without permission in writing from the publisher. Excerpts from
this publication may be reproduced under licence from Access Copyright, or with the
express written permission of Pembroke Publishers Limited, or as permitted by law.

Every effort has been made to contact copyright holders for permission to reproduce
borrowed material. The publishers apologize for any such omissions and will be pleased
to rectify them in subsequent reprints of the book.

We acknowledge the financial support of the Government of Canada through the
Canada Book Fund (CBF) for our publishing activities.

We acknowledge the assistance of the Government of Ontario through the Ontario
Media Development Corporation's Ontario Book Initiative.

Library and Archives Canada Cataloguing in Publication

Paterson, Kathy, author
    3-minute motivators / Kathy Paterson. -- Revised and expanded edition.

Includes bibliographical references and index.
Issued in print and electronic formats.
ISBN 978-1-55138-295-1 (pbk.).--ISBN 978-1-55138-899-1 (pdf)

    1. Effective teaching. 2. Motivation in education. 3. Creative activities and seat work.
I. Title. II. Title: Three-minute motivators.

LB1025.3.P387 2014   371.102   C2014-902868-7
                                             C2014-902869-5

Editor: Kat Mototsune
Cover Design: John Zehethofer
Typesetting: Jay Tee Graphics Ltd.

Printed and bound in Canada
9 8 7 6 5 4 3

FSC
www.fsc.org

MIX
Paper from
responsible sources
FSC® C004071

Contents

Preface to the Revised and Expanded Edition

"Respond; don't react. Listen: don't talk. Think: don't assume."
— Raji Lukkoor, *Inner Pilgrimage: Ten Days to a Mindful Me*

These words provided the foundations of this revised and enhanced version of *3-Minute Motivators*. Using this book, teachers will be responding to, listening to, and thinking about the daily needs of their students to be more in touch, in tune, in step, and in sync with them.

Consider this scenario: At some traffic intersections, loud, flashy barricades drop when trains are near, forcing drivers to stop and wait. When they rise, drivers resume on their way with minimum interruption and maximum safety. But if the barricades failed to fall and drivers failed to stop momentarily, it would lead to disaster! The barricade is a quick time-out. Analogously, 3-Minute Motivators provide these quick time-outs. Each creates a momentary, and often necessary, cessation of focus, without disturbing the overall flow of the classroom.

Daily, we want to encourage intrinsic motivation, manage anxiety, set high goals, and give honest feedback for our students. Sometimes a few moments of off-the-wall fun, energy refocus, or just plain distraction can work wonders in meeting these lofty goals. That's always been the purpose of these quick-fire activities. But I've come to realize that they can do more.

It is obvious that today's students are instantaneously and daily bombarded with sensual stimuli. So is it necessary that their communication be reduced to text messaging? Is it necessary for teachers to resort to only technological devices and media to touch their students? No, definitely not. We know that good teaching is, as always, mandatory for the social, emotional, and intellectual development of youth. And I believe there is a way to be a great teacher with—and perhaps in spite of—technology. That way includes using 3-Minute Motivators as a break from technology.

3-Minute Motivators can also be a tool for management of frustration or stress. In my experience as classroom teacher and instructor of classroom teachers, I have seen many times during the teaching week when the overall mood of the classroom is not as healthy as we would like. This can lead to teacher disillusionment, which in turn can lead to even more antagonistic classroom behaviors. It got me thinking: could a single refocuser make a quick and positive change to that negative situation?

So this new edition of *3-Minute Motivators* not only reworks the tried and true activities of the original book, but also adds new, tech-smart, exhilarating motivators, and explores activities related to mindfulness and wellness. I want it to help teachers by making teaching easier and students more involved, focused, motivated, and self-aware. And I know that this can, in fact, be the case. The following was told to me by a young teacher at a teachers convention in Northern Alberta in 2013. I will not be able to impart the emotion she brought to the story, but I will do my best to repeat her words as accurately as possible:

> 3-Minute Motivators saved my life! I was teaching Junior High for the first time and nothing I did worked. Every lesson bombed. The kids never paid attention. All they wanted to do was talk and fool around or sleep. The Grade 7s were the worst. I dreaded facing them every day and was starting to hate my job. I was ready to quit when a friend gave me a copy of *3-Minute Motivators*. Within a few days—really—things had changed completely. Who knew Grade 7s would love the "Old Duke"? Or would be so involved with "Animal Farm"? Sure surprised me. But it worked. *We* worked! And we laughed together and learned together. I read every single page of that book—it was my go-to friend and it saved my career!

There is nothing in the world so contagious as laughter, smiles, and good humor, and, as this teacher discovered, many of the 3-Minute Motivators capitalize on those aspects of human behavior. In addition, they make use of positive thinking, movement, stillness, silliness, play, communication, cognition, exercise, and mindfulness.

As I began with a quote, let me end with a Swedish proverb:

> Fear less, hope more; Eat less, chew more; Whine less, breathe more; Talk less, say more; Love more, and all good things will be yours.

I hope that this edition of *3-Minute Motivators* will guide all teachers and their students to hope, to breathe, to love, and to learn together.

Introduction

This is a book about magic! As every teacher knows, the best teaching always involves an element of magic—in the persona of the instructor, the presentation of curriculum, or the motivation of the students. Without a touch of magic, teaching can be mundane, students uninspired, lessons less powerful and more forgettable. Think about the following:

Before…
The students are restless. As Ms Black, the teacher, attempts to walk them through the steps for solving the problem, she notes that several are whispering, a couple are daydreaming, another is engaged in annoying the person in front, and most have that familiar vacant "no-one-home" stare. She realizes the brilliant spring sun shining through the window is definitely much more engaging than she is at the moment. She stops talking to see if they will refocus on their own; most don't even seem to notice that she has ceased her presentation.

Teachers will recognize this scenario. It's safe to say that most, if not all, have experienced similar situations and probably are, with increasing frequency, struggling with UUSS—Unmotivated/Unfocused Student Syndrome.

Why? What is making it so difficult for us to reach/teach our students? Is there some way to wake them up, to turn them on, to keep them involved and interested? Is there a secret method for competing with the highly technological worlds of these young people, who are bombarded with sensual stimuli on a daily basis?

Yes, I think there is! Consider this "after" image.

After…
Ms Black shakes her tambourine loudly. All eyes immediately turn to her and talking ceases. Her pre-established and reinforced cue has done its job well. Then she says quietly, "I can see I have lost most of you. Time for a refocuser! Let's play a little game…" The words "play" and "game" invite students' attention. They are familiar with refocusers and enjoy these brief interjections. "Turn to a neighbor," Ms Black continues. "Let's play Shake It!" (See page 69.) Immediately the students are completely engaged in the activity, laughing, talking, and attempting to "shake" the number called by the teacher. After about one minute, Ms Black interrupts the activity by once more shaking the tambourine. "Thanks for stopping on the cue," she says sincerely. "Now that we've shaken out a bit of that excess energy, it's time to return to the problem I was talking to you about…" The students, refocused, return to the task. This time all eyes are on the teacher.

The teacher in this scenario used a little magic to refocus her group; she provided an escape for excess vigor, then efficiently drew the students back into her lesson through a combined process of relaxing and energizing. It is entirely possible—and positive—to be relaxed and energized at the same time. When energy is directed it becomes "quality" energy, and has an innate calming component. As refocusers, 3-Minute Motivators help provide just that. They are simple activities that can be used with any grade, any subject, and any diversity found in the classroom. I have even experienced great success using them with university students and adults at conventions and workshops.

3-Minute Motivators is a collection of these concise activities that can be carried out *at* the desks, *beside* the desks, or *near* the desks, with minimum or no teacher preparation, making use of few props other than the occasional paper and pencil. The actions are designed to involve all the students in interesting, highly motivating ways for approximately three minutes, then to refocus them on the task at hand. Magic!

But why are such activities necessary? Shouldn't students have internal motivation to learn? Shouldn't they want to grow intellectually? Don't they appreciate the personal need for development as human beings? I believe the answer to each question is "yes"; but the many high-level, sense-bombarding, almost mind-numbing distractions in today's society can make classroom learning appear boring, inauthentic, and monotonous.

Consider the students' world. How can children be excited and motivated by what they often see as a dreary and lackluster curriculum, when they are inundated with MP3 players, smart phones, tablets, e-readers, and countless highly technological video games, just to name a few? How can they pay attention to a lesson when they are tempted daily by a wealth of stimulating information at their fingertips via the Internet? How can they sustain single-mindedness for seatwork when they are eager to get back to their camera/game/smart phone/ home entertainment systems?

It takes a touch of magic to keep students inspired and focused today. *3-Minute Motivators* attempts to address this issue by offering a wealth of motivating activities ready for instant use in any classroom. In addition, most of these motivators can be readily adapted to be used as anticipatory sets for a wide variety of lessons. Once you have experimented with a few of them, I think you will agree that they are, indeed, magical. Use them with an open mind; have fun!

3-Minute Motivators in Your Classroom

More Than Just Motivation

"[We can] restore our attention or bring it to a new level by dramatically slowing down whatever is being done." — Sharon Salzberg, *Real Happiness: The Power of Meditation*

Not all of the 3-Minute Motivators in this book are unique. Teachers might be acquainted with some of them. Others might be new ways of looking at familiar activities. But they provide students with something fresh and new. Use them with passion and a sense of humor, and enjoy the positive benefits they bring to the classroom.

What exactly *is* a 3-Minute Motivator? It is a quick activity conducted by the teacher, an activity in which students *want* to participate. Why? Because the words *fun*, *play*, and *game* are integral to the initiating of the motivator. A 3-Minute Motivator redirects energy, allowing the teacher to promptly return to the intended lesson. Whether it involves competition, cooperation, or individual thought or action, the activity provides a much-needed break from an undertaking that has lost the students' interest and attention. And although they might involve considerable physical or mental activity, these activities work toward slowing down non-productive thought processes.

A 3-Minute Motivator is a quick diversion from the task at hand that helps students eliminate less-than-productive behaviors and *refocus* attention back on the lesson. Students themselves quickly come to appreciate and even eagerly anticipate these activities, which can be referred to as *refocusers*. In addition—and this point is of key importance to teachers—all 3-Minute Motivators involve some element of learning in areas including, but not limited to, memory enhancement, creativity, social awareness, personal stress management, mathematical awareness, communication, and wellness. In addition, the motivators in this book can be used as anticipatory sets for lessons in any subject, at any time, and, usually, in any place. Teachers are well aware of the importance of opening lessons with engaging and captivating introductory activities that involve more than students listening to teachers talking. More magic—an entire book of ready-to-go anticipatory sets.

Why use a 3-Minute Motivator?

- To give students a positive break
- To give the teacher a positive break; teachers need breaks too, and these speedy, easy-to-use activities help when they feel they are losing ground.
- To refocus flagging attentions
- To remove excess energy
- To wake up lethargic minds
- To introduce a lesson; most of the activities can have an anticipatory-set function.
- To reward good behavior; they are fun, after all!
- To keep a lesson moving quickly and constructively

As with any good teaching strategies, 3-Minute Motivators all fall within a fairly consistent set of guidelines. For example, they can be satisfactorily completed within a brief amount of time. In addition:

- There are no wrong answers.
- Variety is good and is encouraged.
- All responses are celebrated.
- Private space, both physical and emotional, is always respected.
- The teacher should have fun too.
- Students are allowed the right to pass, or simply sit quietly and watch rather than participate.

Teachers will recognize these as important truths for all teaching, but they need to be reaffirmed with refocusers as they do with other classroom activities.

Inherent Learning

Although 3-Minute Motivators work to refocus attentions, they also speak to a wide variety of teaching/learning situations. In addition, they have inherent learning that, if the teacher chooses, can be elaborated upon. For example, the Shake It! motivator (page 69) indirectly teaches and reinforces the concepts of probability and luck, while providing practice in mentally adding and subtracting, and in cooperating with peers; it could easily be used as an introduction to a lesson on any of these topics. Every one of the refocusers can be broken down into probable learning and a possible focus specific to the curriculum, if so desired.

For example, consider Interactive Words (page 92). Here are just a few areas (there are many more) where this refocuser fits conveniently into a Language Arts program of studies at the Grade 3 level:

- Experimenting with rearranging of material
- Using organizational skills to clarify meaning
- Using a variety of strategies for comprehension
- Extending sight vocabulary
- Applying knowledge of graphologic cueing systems
- Applying word analysis strategies
- Associating sounds with increasing number of vowel combinations
- Applying structural analysis cues
- Explaining relationships among letters in words
- Experimenting with words
- Using phonics knowledge
- Speaking and reading with fluency, rhythm, pace
- Working cooperatively with others

Another way to use these specific motivators is as quick anticipatory sets for appropriate lessons. For example, Shake It (page 69) could be used effectively prior to a math class on addition, subtraction, or fractions. Synonym Sense (page 110) might make a motivating anticipatory set for a Language Arts lesson on descriptive writing or vocabulary development.

Now consider the same motivator from the point of view of students' inherent learning. While participating in Interactive Words, it is quite possible that many, if not all, of them would learn, quite naturally, the following:

- Words can be broken into parts.
- Letters all have unique sounds.
- Letter combinations have unique sounds and often unique meanings.
- Big words often contain smaller words within them.
- Chanting words one letter at a time helps with spelling.
- Chanting with peers is fun and helps with memory.

Another way to consider the importance of 3-Minute Motivators is to think of them as teachable moments. All teachers are familiar with these as often the very best opportunities to reach and teach.

No doubt this same motivator could be examined successfully from the standpoint of other core subject curricula as well. It is always good for teachers to know that what they are doing is not only highly motivating, but also is viable as far as teaching to the existing program of studies. There is definitely incidental inherent learning involved.

Choosing the Right 3-Minute Motivator

Teachers can simply select an activity at random. For example, the math class is "lost" and completely disengaged—a refocuser is called for! The book opens to Word Tennis (page 112) and in less than 60 seconds all students are busily tossing math words back and forth between partners. A random choice proves effective nonetheless.

Using this book is primarily a matter of choosing the best activity for any given moment and situation.

All teachers are fully aware of the importance of purpose when teaching. It is mandatory for a teacher—and even students—to know *why* something is being presented, reviewed, or taught. The same goes for using 3-Minute Motivators. Quickly deciding why one of them is about to be used can be a determining factor in selecting the best motivator. Is it just to refocus the students, or is another purpose, like lesson introduction, to be met at the same time? Certainly the single act of refocusing students so that a lesson can begin or be continued is significant, and often sufficient; however, teachers usually want to meet as many requirements as possible with every classroom action.

With this in mind, the question arises: "Aren't all 3-Minute Motivators mainly designed to motivate?" Yes, but student distractions can present as restlessness, hyperactivity, fatigue, or apathy (to name a few). Moreover, many other variables come into play, such as the time of day or week, the subject being interrupted by the motivator, or the teacher stance (i.e., current level of patience, acceptance, or frustration). Therefore, the choice of the best motivator becomes a bit more difficult.

Skim or scan the activities described in the different sections, highlight or tab the ones you find the most interesting and relevant to your students' ages, needs, etc. Keep the book readily available for instant access. You don't even have to think of what to say—just open at a tab and read the italicized words.

Teachers might, for example, be faced with students who are vacant and sleepy-looking; they can choose a motivator that will "wake up" students and provide the jolt of energy necessary to complete the assignment or lesson. Or a teacher might want to get students communicating prior to a Social Studies discussion and, perhaps because it is Friday afternoon and raining outside, the children are noisy, out-of-seat, and restless—in this case a motivator that involves sitting and speaking could be what is required. Or the teacher might perceive growing classroom anxiety, or worry, or fearfulness (e.g., prior to a test), or escalating annoyance or even anger (e.g., following some upset in expected routine) in students. If this is the case, one of the quickies from Stress Attack (page 147) might not only defuse the situation, but also provide students with a tool they can use elsewhere in their lives.

To simplify the process of finding the right motivator for any situation, the activities have been organized into groups, and then further specified as types. For example, the At Your Desks group of motivators all require the minimum of physical movement and are divided into two types: Calm Down motivators involve being still and thinking (see page 24); Pencil and Paper activities have the students using these tools to complete the tasks (see page 37). For descriptions of the motivators in the Up and At 'Em group of more action-oriented activities, see page 53 for the Get Active type, page 65 for the Get Involved type, and page 77 for the Sound and Movement type. 3-Minute Motivators in the Let's Communicate group are divided into types that focus on Single Words and Sounds (page 90), Conversation (page 98), and Brainstorm (page 107). See page 119 for motivators can be used as extended activities that go Beyond the Three-Minute Mark, highly engaging yet learning-packed activities that can be integrated into daily routines. Finally, the Today and Tomorrow chapter includes motivators that include and address digital skills through Digital Fingertips and Digital Desks in Tech Too (page 139), and activities that establish and enhance life skills in Stress Attack (page 147).

See chart on pages 19–22.

When choosing a 3-Minute Motivator out of the 217 in this book, your best tool might be the 3-Minute Motivators at a Glance table on pages 19–22. A quick scan of the table will give you an idea of the nature of each motivator and any particular subjects it might be most useful to address.

Suggested Subject(s)

Many of the activities are more appropriate for one subject or another, so Subject(s) have been listed both in the 3-Minute Motivators at a Glance table (pages 19–22) and on each activity. While not intended to limit use of any specific motivator to the subject(s) suggested, the labels indicate the subject most likely addressed.

Many motivators have no specific subject affinity, or have a cross-curricular nature; this is indicated by the subject label *Any*.

Noteworthy is the fact that all the activities involve some sort of communication, and all address most strands of the Language Arts curriculum.

If, for example, the teacher wants to use a motivator during a Science lesson, and doesn't want students to lose the "Science" train of thought, a logical choice might be an activity with a *Science* label attached. Keep in mind, however, that any motivator can be used with, or during, any subject.

Number of Students

The motivators are categorized as *Individual*, *Partners*, *Small Group*, or *Whole Class*, allowing teachers to narrow their choices. If students are being too social, for example, perhaps a motivator listed as *Individual* would be more effective than one that involves partner or small-group work.

When having students find partners or form small groups, it is often most expedient to have "neighbors" or students adjacent to each other work together. Since the activity is very brief, taking a long time to form partners or groups defeats the purpose. However, teachers might want to mix things up by suggesting other ways of forming pairs/groups, as unusual groupings can be advantageous and the low-risk nature of the activities facilitates this kind of grouping.

3-Minute Motivators that are performed alone by each student, without conferring in any way with peers, are listed as *Individual*. Some activities have individual students adding to, being a part of, or helping to complete a task that involves the whole class; these motivators are labeled *Individual as part of Whole Class*. 3-Minute Motivators that have students working in pairs are listed as *Partners*. In some instances, partners work together to compete with the whole class, challenging other pairs in a competitive way; these activities are labeled *Partners as part of Whole Class*.

Keep in mind that these labels are just suggestions; most motivators can be altered to work individually or otherwise.

Props and Prep

There are a few 3-Minute Motivators that are accompanied by illustrations. They are included as teacher examples, to help clarify the activities, but can be shared with the class in the form of overheads or interactive whiteboard visuals, if desired.

A part of your choice of activity might be whether or not you need to acquire and distribute materials to use, and if the activity requires preparation. The props can be as simple as a piece of paper and writing tool but, if speed is important, even the handing out of materials or the act of students getting them ready might make a particular motivator inappropriate for the specific time. For this reason, if props or other prep are required, they are listed in the chart on pages 19–22.

A few of the 3-Minute Motivators suggest the use of music props. The music usually referred to is of the slow, calming genre often found as yoga, relaxation, or environmental music. Even some classical music will work. The key is to keep the music soft and soothing, so it operates in the background to set mood. Be sure the music has no lyrics. Please note, however, that with the exception of Hearing Colors (page 26), all motivators will work well without music.

Other props are as simple as a coin or flash cards. Prop labels have been used to simplify your choice. In a hurry? Avoid an activity with a prop. Or have an aid, volunteer, or older student create the props or prep for you ahead of time.

Extending the Activities

Debrief and Showcase sections are provided for some activities. A note to Debrief means that the activity is a good one for a brief follow-up discussion. To keep within the 3-Minute part of the definition (necessary if lesson flow is to be maintained), a 60-second "discuss with a neighbor" is suggested.

If the motivator outlines an Extended Debrief, it indicates that an activity that will work well with a longer, more in-depth discussion, and perhaps lead to writing (e.g., journal reflection, story starter, sequenced directions) or representation (e.g., creating a poster or visual, puppet presentation, drama skit). I have listed proposals for some of these Extended Debriefs, but they are merely suggestions. No one knows your class better than you, and your ideas for Extended Debriefs are limitless.

A few 3-Minute Motivators include suggestions for Showcase, indicating that the activity could be shared with peers. The Showcase can be as simple as 30 seconds for students to show the rest of the class the products of their activity, or as elaborate as sharing with other classes and parents as part of an open house or concert. Often children enjoy showing off something they feel is cool or amusing, so why not encourage their natural desire to let others see what they have done? The time allowed for a Showcase should fall within the three-minute proscription—we're talking about a quick, snappy sharing here. Not all students will be able to showcase every time, so you will need to be aware of turn-taking and equal opportunity. If everyone wants to showcase a particular activity, the best approach would be to point out that you will share when the interrupted lesson has been completed, to avoid losing the flow of the lesson.

3-Minute Motivators in Action

Once you have chosen a 3-Minute Motivator, take a few minutes first to browse the contents. Note that your spoken directions, the words you will say to the students, are presented in *italics*. Oral directions are presented in this manner to expedite presentation—all you need to do is read the brief notes to the class—and keep the motivators simple and quick to use. Naturally, the directions provided do not need to be used word-for-word; they are guidelines only. A quick read of the entire motivator will probably be sufficient for instant use.

All teachers speak for a living, so express the instructions, directions, and invitations to "play" enthusiastically, with the intent to stimulate. Put a smile in your voice and a twinkle in your eye. Be one of those people who can make anything sound exciting by using voice tone, quality, and modulation. Use direct language (e.g., "We will take part in a fun activity..."), because indirect phrasing (e.g., "Do you want to take part in...") invites negative responses. Finally, maintain eye contact and make use of the powerful pregnant pause; for example, "We are going to take part in a fun activity...(pause for about 5 seconds)...called Number Shakes."

When using an Extended Debrief at the end of a 3-Minute Motivator, say, "Remember what you just did/thought/said/visualized, and we'll come back to that after we finish our lesson." The motivator is not intended to replace the lesson, but to refocus attention to it. Returning to the activity when the lesson is over, for an extended debrief, is a teachable moment.

Some of the 3-Minute Motivators make use of lists of ideas, word combinations, situations, themes, etc. Because I often found it difficult to generate inventories on the spur of the moment, I came to depend on previously prepared lists. You could keep such lists on your computer or on file cards on your desk. Throughout this book you will find a number of such ready-to-go lists.

When introducing a 3-Minute Motivator to your class, for the first time or the fiftieth time, it is good to reinforce these ideas:

- There is no wrong answer.
- Variety is good.
- All responses are celebrated.
- Private space, both physical and emotional, is always respected.

You will find that after a couple of uses, you will memorize the directions you give for any 3-Minute Motivator.

Any non-italicized text within the activity steps (presented as a bulleted list) supplies additional directions. It might, for example, suggest that you "cue to start," or "remind students when they have 30 seconds remaining." Unlike the italicized words, these are not meant to be read explicitly to the class.

Use the full list of steps on page 23 as a handy reference for using a 3-Minute Motivator. It includes the entire process, from Attention Cue to Concluding and Refocusing back on the lesson.

The Attention Cue

High Priority!

As every teacher knows, if the students aren't attending, the teacher isn't teaching. So it is with 3-Minute Motivators. The students must be paying attention when we introduce the activity. But it's because the students are *not* attending that a 3-Minute Motivator is needed in the first place. So we must make them voluntarily pay attention by doing something so attractive, different, or out-of-character that they have to sit up and take notice. We *cue!* The cue can be a sound (e.g., a whistle), a visual (e.g., standing on a chair), a smell (e.g., a blast of room spray)—but it must be dynamic. As a rule, establish the attention cue prior to the use of any 3-Minute Motivator—you likely already have attention cues in place. To begin a refocuser, use an attention cue that has worked for you in the past.

All teachers have their own cues, but here are a few snappy ones I have witnessed working well:

- a short blast of a whistle, a blare of child's plastic horn (check dollar stores for party favors), or a shake of a tambourine
- a rhythm band instrument
- a specific piece of music played loudly
- a clapping sequence led by you (This is particularly good if you are clapping two loud objects, such as sticks or tin lids, together.)
- raising your hand and waiting silently until all students have hands raised
- whispering—yes, really—something to a student near you, who whispers it to another, and so on (You will need something important to whisper, such as the answer to a question, or a joke or riddle.)
- vigorously engaging a New Years Eve noisemaker
- rapping a squeaky hammer (or anything resembling a gavel) on your desk (This is my personal favorite, as it simulates a courtroom with the teacher as judge. My huge squeaky hammer works well with students at *any* level— even adult students!)

An exciting attention cue is quickly inflating a balloon then letting it go. As it zips noisily around the room, all eyes are focused and the teacher has the floor! But this can be used only once or maybe twice.

As with any situation in which a specific reaction is expected to a specific cue, the use of the cue must be first introduced, then cultivated and reinforced. These steps are vital to the success of any cueing, and therefore the success of 3-Minute Motivators:

1. Introduce the cue and explain its purpose.
   When you hear this noise, you will immediately stop what you are doing and look at me.
2. Practice.
   Everybody talk to a neighbor and be prepared to freeze when you hear this noise.
3. Reinforce.

- *Excellent! You all stopped talking and looked at me. That's exactly what I wanted you to do. This helps me because…*
- *I'm so glad you all remembered to freeze on cue and look at me. Now I know you are ready to…*
- *Thank you for freezing when you heard the cue. That's great! I know you want to…*

Repeat steps 2 and 3 frequently for the first few days, reinforcing consistently. Eventually, obeying the attention cue should become a classroom habit and can be reinforced intermittently.

The Importance of Concluding and Refocusing

Perhaps the most important aspect of successfully using a 3-Minute Motivator is the manner in which it is ended. A smooth transition is a step necessary to enabling the teacher to bring the class back from an activity to the previously interrupted task or lesson. Although it takes only a few moments to make this crucial shift in focus, without it, students might be left wondering what they just did, why they did it, and where they are supposed to be going as a result.

Once the motivator is finished to your satisfaction,

1. Cue for attention.
2. Quickly verbalize why the refocuser/motivator was carried out.
   I had the feeling none of you were really listening to the information about _____, so we (summarize the activity).
3. Concisely state current expectations for return to work.
   Now that you've had a chance to burn some energy (talk to a neighbor, move around a bit, etc.), I need you to return to the lesson and give it your full attention.
4. Provide positive reinforcement for return-to-work behaviors
5. Continue with the lesson or remind students what they were supposed to be doing pre-motivator.
   We were learning about_____ and I was explaining how to…

Concluding a 3-Minute Motivator follows a what–why–what pattern: *what* was done, *why* it was done, *what* will happen next.

This entire "speech" should take no more than 30 seconds. Students will quickly learn that, although they have fun with the motivators, they are expected to return to work immediately following them.

Class Participation

If some students are reluctant to cooperate and participate, even when the activity is presented as a game, allow them to choose to sit quietly at their desks and simply observe. It has been my experience that, after one or two times just observing, most students want to take part in activities, especially those that allow them imaginative freedom. On the other hand, many of the 3-Minute Motivators are entertaining to watch, and less-outgoing students might choose to enjoy them from this point of view; they still benefit from the refocusing quality of the motivator.

Your main difficulty might be with students who wish to disrupt the class during the more quiet activities. The very nature of the Calm Down 3-Minute Motivators will be jeopardized if even a single student is noisy. You must deal with these situations in whatever way works best for you, keeping in mind that the success of calming activities depends on a room that is quiet for up to three minutes. If the student cannot or will not meet the three-minute criterion, it might be best to remove him or her for the short duration of the activity.

Tips for Teaching with 3-Minute Motivators

- Make it fun, not punishment! Better to say, "Time for a refocuser. This is a little game…" than to say, "No one is on task and you are all talking, so we have to do something to change that…" The word *game* is the catch for kids.
- Always begin with your pre-established attention cue and end with a return to the interrupted or ensuing lesson.
- Always tell students *why* you have chosen to have them participate in a 3-Minute Motivator.
- Stick to the three-minute time frame as much as possible (unless you have a reason for varying the process). If you wish to debrief a motivator, keep it to about one minute, or say, "Remember what you just did/thought/saw /heard… and we'll talk about it after we finish our…(whatever you interrupted)."
- Use the term *refocuser* when referring to 3-Minute Motivators. The jargony term appeals to kids, and they start to look forward to the chance to "refocus."
- Remember the element of surprise. Keep your motivators fresh. Avoid using the same one over and over, and choose activities from different sections regularly. Mix them up.
- Note that directions for the teacher to say/read in *italics* mean that a motivator can be used instantaneously if necessary.
- It's a good idea to familiarize yourself with a few activities from each section, but don't feel you need to memorize the teacher's speaking directions.
- Don't feel forced to read class instructions exactly as they are written. The scripts are guidelines only. You will certainly add your own flavor and make the motivators your own.
- Be sure the directions you provide (following the attention cue) are specific and exact. Remember that you want to reduce chaos, not create it.
- Use 3-Minute Motivators proactively rather than reactively. It is better to stop the lesson and interject a motivator when behaviors are just starting to wane, than when behaviors have escalated to the classroom bedlam all teachers face from time to time.
- Realize that Debrief, Extended Debrief, and Showcase prompts are suggestions only; you can choose to use them or ignore them.
- Realize that, although a motivator might call for props, it will often work well without them.
- Don't worry if a motivator bombs! Just admit defeat and return to the lesson. (Even a bombing activity serves, in its own way, to refocus.)
- Keep a record (perhaps using the 3-Minute Motivators at a Glance table on pages 19–22) of motivators that you have used effectively or ineffectively, that you would like to use again or would prefer to forget. Since the book contains so many motivators, this simple bookkeeping will simplify future use of the activities.

What About Competition and Prizes?

Remember that mild competition is motivating and can be a useful tool, but is to be used at the teacher's discretion.

3-Minute Motivators can be used competitively or noncompetitively. Some motivators lend themselves to unusual competitive challenges: these can be enhanced with the addition of small prizes. It is not the size or quality of the prize that counts, but rather the *idea* of the prize that is, in itself, motivating. What's magical about many of the prizes associated with 3-Minute Motivators is that they are often won by students who seldom excel in other classroom pursuits. Here are some suggestions for quick prizes that are easy to obtain and store:

- small, individually wrapped candy; e.g., Halloween candy
- boxes of raisins
- fortune cookies
- party favors; i.e., from dollar or party stores
- stickers put on students' hands
- stamps put on students' hands
- stars—all ages; the bigger the better!

3-Minute Motivators at a Glance

Suggested Subject: Any (with no specific subject affinity)

MOTIVATOR	PROPS	PREP
5. Imagine This		
7. Chocolate and Bricks		
8. Pop-a-lot	✓	✓
9. Grounding Exercise		
12. Absolutely Nothing!		
24. Box Me In	✓	
26. O's and X's	✓	
29. Word Lotto	✓	
30. Thinking Cap	✓	
39. Scrabble Scramble	✓	
41. Snowglobe Drawings	✓	
48. Open–Shut–Shake		
55. Cold–Hot–Not	✓	✓
57. False Freeze	✓	
59. Bump on the Head		
61. Wide–Hide		
69. All Shook Up	✓	
72. Monkey See, Monkey Do		
73. Body by Color		
74. Musical Punching Bags		
75. Shake It!		
81. Do This! Do That!		
91. Move It		
92. Walk This Way		
93. Wrangle Tangle		
94. Explosion	✓	✓
95. The Old Duke Revisited		
97. Meet and Greet		

MOTIVATOR	PROPS	PREP
100. Kodak Moments		
104. Chain Spell		
108. Talk-a-lot		
109. Gibberish		
111. Interactive Words		
117. Popcorn		
118. Alphabet Pyramid		
121. Quick Catch		
124. Alphabet Speak		
125. Slow-mo		
126. A Quantity of Questions		
128. People Who…		✓
129. You DON'T Say!		
132. Fortunately/Unfortunately		
134. May There Be…		
136. Hi–Lo Speak		
138. I Am!		✓
142. Synonym Sense		✓
143. Go-Togethers		✓
144. Word Tennis		
147. Mystery Word		✓
148. Quick Questions		✓
149. Under the Umbrella		✓
151. Excuses, Excuses		✓
153. Word Expansion		✓
154. If They Could Talk		✓
156. Over/Under		
157. Cloze It		✓
159. Obstacle Course		
166. Sense or Nonsense?		✓
172. Passion Poem		✓
182. The Unfair Test		✓

MOTIVATOR	PROPS	PREP
184. Twinkle Twinkle	✓	
185. Nibbles	✓	
186. Rockin' Rice Balls	✓	✓
187. Fact or Fiction		✓
188. Then & Now		✓
189. The Good, the Bad, and the Really Awful		
190. Tech Search	✓	
191. Going Back	✓	
192. Tech Cross		✓
193. Unusual & Unique		✓

Suggested Subject: Art

MOTIVATOR	PROPS	PREP
3. Hearing Colors	✓	
4. Magic Carpet		
20. Bubble Brigade	✓	✓
21. Scribble, Crumple & Tear	✓	
22. Zen Garden	✓	
27. Two-Centimetre Trail	✓	
31. Never-ending Line	✓	
32. Draw My Words	✓	
45. Scribble People	✓	
46. Sign Me a Picture	✓	
78. Blind Walk	✓	
79. Teddy or Grizzly		
80. Morphing Madness		
84. Lump of Clay		
100. Kodak Moments		
174. A-One Superhero	✓	
177. Beautiful People	✓	

Suggested Subject: **Health & Wellness**

MOTIVATOR	PROPS	PREP
1. Belly Breathing		
3. Hearing Colors	✓	
7. Chocolate and Bricks		
10. Hug a Tree		
11. Silent Scream		
15. Featherweight Arms		
19. Fun School Facts	✓	
20. Bubble Brigade	✓	✓
21. Scribble, Crumple & Tear	✓	
22. Zen Garden	✓	
23. One-Minute Memory	✓	
36. Teddy Bear or Tiger	✓	
38. My Up, My Down	✓	
40. Blind Draw	✓	
47. The Happy Gratefuls	✓	
51. Life Rhythms		
53. Blasting Balloons	✓	
64. Fast Feet		
65. In Your Arms		
82. As the Circle Turns		
83. Lean on Me		
88. Sourpuss		
89. Going Noisily Nowhere		
90. Ages of Humanity		
96. Walk or Block		
97. Meet and Greet		
98. If You're Happy…		
114. Chant-along	✓	
123. I Am You		
130. "Yes, But" Pet Peeves		
131. Glad Game		
133. I Appreciate…Because	✓	
137. Poor Me!		
146. Rephrase/Reframe/Refresh		✓
161. Give Me a Clue		✓

Suggested Subject: **Language Arts**

MOTIVATOR	PROPS	PREP
4. Magic Carpet		
13. The Key		
15. Featherweight Arms		
18. Joke in a Jar	✓	✓
19. Fun School Facts	✓	
23. One-Minute Memory	✓	
28. Letter Scramble	✓	
32. Draw My Words	✓	
34. Written Rumor	✓	
35. Shared-Pen Stories	✓	
36. Teddy Bear or Tiger	✓	
38. My Up, My Down	✓	
39. Scrabble Scramble	✓	
40. Blind Draw	✓	
42. Mirror Images	✓	
43. Air Writing	✓	
44. Line Challenge	✓	
45. Scribble People	✓	
46. Sign Me a Picture	✓	
47. The Happy Gratefuls	✓	
49. Puppet Master		
53. Blasting Balloons	✓	
60. Knocking Knees		
63. Ice Cube		
65. In Your Arms		
77. Tap It to Me	✓	
88. Sourpuss		
90. Ages of Humanity		
91. Move It		
96. Walk or Block		
97. Meet and Greet		
99. Mad Milling		
100. Kodak Moments		
101. The Shape You're In		
102. Pied Piper		
103. Blast Off!		
104. Chain Spell		
105. Beat Reading	✓	✓
106. Hummingbirds and Crows		
107. Same Make, Same Model		
109. Gibberish		
110. Oscar	✓	✓
111. Interactive Words		
113. Hip-hip-hooray		
114. Chant-along	✓	✓
116. Punctuate This!	✓	✓
118. Alphabet Pyramid		
120. The Numbered Letter		
122. Song Speak		
124. Alphabet Speak		
127. You Did What?		
130. "Yes, But" Pet Peeves		
135. Third-Person Talk		
137. Poor Me!		
139. Times-10 Tales		
140. Point Please?	✓	✓
141. And the Real Meaning Is…		
142. Synonym Sense	✓	
144. Word Tennis		
145. Transform It	✓	
146. Rephrase/Reframe/Refresh	✓	
150. Big Word/Small Word	✓	
152. Break-up	✓	
153. Word Expansion	✓	
155. First and Last		
157. Cloze It	✓	✓
158. Oxy-challenge	✓	
160. Let's Quiggle		
161. Give Me a Clue		✓
162. Specifics, Please	✓	✓
163. The Rule Rules!		
165. Tell It Like It Is		✓
166. Sense or Nonsense?	✓	✓
167. It's MY Story!		
168. The Expert	✓	✓
169. And the Action Is…		
170. Forever After		
171. ScraPPle	✓	✓
172. Passion Poem	✓	
173. Action Telephone	✓	✓
174. A-One Superhero	✓	
175. Toilet Tales	✓	
176. Fortuneteller	✓	
177. Beautiful People	✓	✓
178. My Favorite Letter	✓	
179. I Know You!	✓	
180. I Could Live Without It		
181. Unusual Uses	✓	
183. Two Truths and a Lie		

Suggested Subject: **Life Skills**

MOTIVATOR	PROPS	PREP
200. Forced Smile		
201. Fake Yawn		
202. Loud Silence		
203. Flip It in Color		
204. Lung Bellows		
205. The Effort/Achievement Connection		
206. Tap Technique		
207. Ear Yoga		
208. Finger Focus		
209. Focus Fix		
210. Toe Wiggles		
211. Chew Too	✓	
212. Back Up		
213. Face It		
214. Stand Tall		

215. Sky Reaching
216. Wall Pushing
217. Chest Opening

Suggested Subject: **Math**

MOTIVATOR	PROPS	PREP
15. Featherweight Arms		
25. Circles & Squares	✓	
31. Never-ending Line	✓	
33. Number Madness	✓	
34. Written Rumor	✓	
42. Mirror Images	✓	
43. Air Writing	✓	
58. Balancing Act		
62. Heads or Tails	✓	
66. Circles, Circles, Circles		
68. Number Shakes		
71. Lucky Hi/Lo	✓	
72. Monkey See, Monkey Do		
85. Shake My Hand	✓	✓
86. Beanbag Blitz	✓	
101. The Shape You're In		
103. Blast Off!		
112. Count-off		
118. Alphabet Pyramid		
119. Clap 3		
120. The Numbered Letter		
160. Let's Quiggle		
161. Give Me a Clue		✓
162. Specifics, Please	✓	✓
163. The Rule Rules!		
164. Back Talk	✓	✓
178. My Favorite Letter	✓	

Suggested Subject: **Musics**

MOTIVATOR	PROPS	PREP
60. Knocking Knees		
98. If You're Happy…		
122. Song Speak		

Suggested Subject: **Phys Ed**

MOTIVATOR	PROPS	PREP
51. Life Rhythms		
58. Balancing Act		
64. Fast Feet		
66. Circles, Circles, Circles		
78. Blind Walk	✓	
79. Teddy or Grizzly		
80. Morphing Madness		

83. Lean on Me
86. Beanbag Blitz ✓
87. Glued to the Ground
89. Going Noisily Nowhere
91. Move It
92. Walk This Way
93. Wrangle Tangle
98. If You're Happy…

Suggested Subject: **Research**

MOTIVATOR	PROPS	PREP
187. Fact or Fiction		✓
188. Then & Now		✓
189. The Good, the Bad, and the Really Awful		
190. Tech Search	✓	
191. Going Back		✓
192. Tech Cross	✓	
193. Unusual & Unique		✓
194. I Web 2.0 Too		

Suggested Subject: **Science**

MOTIVATOR	PROPS	PREP
2. Collecting Clouds	✓	
6. Time Machine		
10. Hug a Tree		
14. Lift Off!		
15. Featherweight Arms		
16. Catitude		
17. Telescope		
19. Fun School Facts	✓	
20. Bubble Brigade	✓	✓
21. Scribble, Crumple & Tear	✓	
25. Circles & Squares	✓	
27. Two-Centimetre Trail	✓	
31. Never-ending Line	✓	
32. Draw My Words	✓	
37. Zoom Out	✓	
42. Mirror Images	✓	
43. Air Writing	✓	
44. Line Challenge	✓	
50. Glass Blower		
52. Thunderstorm		
56. Stuck!		
58. Balancing Act		
63. Ice Cube		
64. Fast Feet		
65. In Your Arms		
66. Circles, Circles, Circles		

67. Melt
70. Balloon Battles ✓
76. Magic Mirrors ✓
78. Blind Walk ✓
79. Teddy or Grizzly
80. Morphing Madness
85. Shake My Hand ✓ ✓
86. Beanbag Blitz ✓
87. Glued to the Ground
91. Move It
101. The Shape You're In
102. Pied Piper
103. Blast Off!
106. Hummingbirds and Crows
107. Same Make, Same Model
115. Animal Farm
117. Popcorn
145. Transform It ✓
160. Let's Quiggle
161. Give Me a Clue ✓
162. Specifics, Please ✓ ✓
163. The Rule Rules!
168. The Expert ✓ ✓
169. And the Action Is…
170. Forever After
174. A-One Superhero ✓
176. Fortuneteller ✓
181. Unusual Uses ✓

Suggested Subject: **Social Studies**

MOTIVATOR	PROPS	PREP
11. Silent Scream		
40. Blind Draw	✓	
44. Line Challenge	✓	
47. The Happy Gratefuls	✓	
49. Puppet Master		
50. Glass Blower		
69. All Shook Up	✓	✓
85. Shake My Hand	✓	✓
96. Walk or Block		
97. Meet and Greet		
99. Mad Milling		
101. The Shape You're In		
102. Pied Piper		
103. Blast Off!		
106. Hummingbirds and Crows		
107. Same Make, Same Model		
122. Song Speak		
123. I Am You		
133. I Appreciate…Because	✓	

Suggested Subject: **Technology**

MOTIVATOR	PROPS	PREP
195. Tech Tennis		
196. Tech-sion		
197. Tech Alpha-talk		
198. Need-an-App	✓	
199. Once It Was…	✓	

Steps for Using a 3-Minute Motivator

1. Cue to gain attention. *High Priority!*

2. Briefly explain why the motivator is being used.

   I have lost you…
   You seem restless…
   I can see you need a break…
   You seem to need some talk time…
   I feel like I'm getting nowhere here…

3. Explain the activity, using the directions included in each 3-Minute Motivator.

4. Remind students not to begin until you cue them to, and to stop or freeze again on cue.

5. Cue to begin.

6. Present the 3-Minute Motivator, using the script provided.

7. Cue to stop.

8. Conclude and refocus by quickly summarizing what was done and why.

   We were all a bit restless so we just played _____. Now that you've used up a bit of energy, it's time to return to…

   You seemed sleepy and many of you were not paying attention, so we played _____. Now that you're all awake, let's get back to…

   I felt the need for a quick break, so we played _____. Now we can get back to…

© 2014 *3-Minute Motivators* by Kathy Paterson. Pembroke Publishers. ISBN 978-1-55138-295-1

At Your Desks

All 3-Minute Motivators in this chapter are carried out at students' desks or tables, so no great movements or crowd-control methods are required. These refocusers are designed to reduce off-task behaviors from distractedness or lack of interest, and thereby also reduce stress.

Calm Down

"When we teach a child patience we offer them the gift of a dignified life. Patience requires a slowing down, a spaciousness, a sense of self." — Allan Lokos, *Patience: The Art of Peaceful Living*

The motivators in this section require the least amount of physical activity, as students remain seated silently at their desks throughout. With the teacher leading, students engage their imaginations in interesting, often unusual, ways. That these refocusing activities involve a degree of meditation, of quiet reflection and rumination, of slowing down and breathing, will quickly become obvious to you. What might be less obvious is how successfully students of all ages can handle, learn from, and appreciate such deliberations.

These refocusers are most effective for situations in which students have been very active; the teacher's goal is to calm them down in preparation for a more concentrated pursuit. For example, students might be off-task, talkative, out-of-desk, non-focused, or actively uninterested in the lesson or job at hand. There might be a general state of disorganization or hyperactivity in the room, or simply too much contagious energy to allow for effective teaching and subsequent learning to take place.

- To capitalize on the intention of relaxation, use a quiet, soothing, often monotone voice when providing the direction or presenting the scenarios. This is not a time for high passion and enthusiasm, but for a firm, tranquil, and composed intervention.
- Some of these calming motivators (Belly Breathing, Hug-a-Tree, Grounding Exercise, Zen Garden) work well before important or intense seatwork activity, such as an exam. They can serve to reduce anxiety and encourage maximum effort.
- Most of the refocusers in this section take the form of "guided imagery," as the teacher calmly guides the thinking and internal visualization of the students. If some students reject this type of imagery, at least they will be sitting quietly with their eyes closed for the duration, and that in itself can serve as a positive experience.
- Most of these motivators work best on an individual basis; however, you might wish to debrief by encouraging quiet discussion between students or individual journalling of thoughts/feelings as natural follow-ups.

- The opportunities for authentic question/answer sessions or in-depth follow-up writing like essays are many, even if the particular refocuser does not include Debrief or Showcase notes. Neither of these literacy activities will lessen the effectiveness of the relaxing refocuser.
- A few of these refocusers (Joke in a Jar, Fun School Facts) require some preparation; i.e., collecting jokes/facts/trivia, having them written on cards or slips of paper, and placing them in a readily available container. See margin notes on Prep for these activities.

Calm Down

Subject: Health & Wellness

Individual

Note: Belly Breathing can be used *before* other motivators in this section, as an additional calming activity.

1. Belly Breathing

Objective: To breathe deeply with patience and control.

- *Sit quietly at your desk, hands folded.*
- *Close your eyes.*
- *Breathe normally.*
- *Now focus on your breathing: slowly* in *to a count of 5, hold for 5, slowly* out *for a count of 5.*
- *When you inhale, visualize yourself getting bigger and lighter. Air is rushing in to fill all your body cavities: chest, stomach, back, shoulders...*
- *When you hold your breath, visualize yourself getting lighter and lighter, even levitating.*
- *When you exhale, visualize yourself squeezing your lungs, getting rid of every bit of air, pushing it all out through your mouth. (This might make you cough, and that's okay. It just means you are getting all the dead air out.)*
- *Be patient with yourself; slow your breathing.*
- Remind students to keep their eyes closed, to continue breathing like this for about two minutes, and to silently count the seconds to themselves. Talk about "filling up like a balloon" when inhaling, and "squeezing your diaphragm down to your hips and sucking your tummy in" when exhaling.
- Allow students to continue for as long as they remain focused, or up to a maximum of two minutes, then say,
- *This will be your last breath. Slowly fill yourself up, count. Exhale and, as you curl down into yourself like a balloon losing all its air, you feel quiet, calm, relaxed...*

Calm Down

Subject: Science

Individual

Prop: Calming music for yoga, environmental sounds, relaxation CDs

2. Collecting Clouds

Objective: To attain a sense of calm by visualizing clouds.

- *Sit comfortably, feet on floor, heads on desks, arms comfortably wherever you want them*
- *Close your eyes and focus on your breathing.* Allow about 15 seconds for this.
- *Now, think of clouds—a beautiful clear blue sky and lots of clouds.*
- *What do your clouds look like? See them in your mind. Really look at them. What shapes are they? Are they changing shape? Are they moving?*
- *Imagine you are floating on one of the clouds, sinking into it and being surrounded by it. What does it feel like? What can you see?*
- Allow this to continue silently for up to 30 seconds or until you note restlessness, then continue:
- *Now come back down to earth, but keep feeling the gentle movement of the clouds as you sit up quietly.*

Extended Debrief: Pre-writing, illustrating, etc.

Showcase: Sharing of extended debrief products.

Calm Down

Subjects: Art; Health & Wellness

Individual

Prop: Calming music for yoga, environmental sounds, relaxation CDs, even classical music

3. Hearing Colors

Objective: To attach imaginary colors to sounds.

- *Sit quietly at your desk, feet on the floor, heads on desktops. Close your eyes.*
- *You are going to hear some music. Listen to it and see in your mind the colors the music makes you think of.*
- Play the music. Wait for 10 seconds then say, *What colors do you see? Does the music make you think of green? Or maybe pink? Concentrate on the colors of the rainbow and try to visualize which shades this music makes you think of. Breathe deeply and think color.*
- *I am going to stop the music. When I do, you will sit up quietly and think of the color or colors you saw in your mind.*

Debrief: Students can quietly share visualized colors; or you can conduct a quick survey of the predominant colors.

Calm Down

Subjects: Language Arts; Art
Individual

4. Magic Carpet

Objective: To experience sensory awareness.

- *Sit quietly, feet on floor, head on hands on desk. Close your eyes and breathe deeply.*
- *I am going to take you away from here on a magic-carpet ride. Imagine you are not sitting in your desk; you are on a beautiful carpet. Think these things in your mind: "What does your carpet look like? What color is it? What does it feel like?"*
- *Now the carpet is going to start moving. It is slowly rising up, slowly, rising…getting higher. What does it feel like now? Pay attention to the feel of it underneath you. Can you feel the gentle movement? Pay attention to the gentle breeze in your face as your special carpet moves higher and higher.*
- *You feel very comfortable. You are high above the clouds. You are totally relaxed as your carpet sails along like a bird in the air.*
- *Now imagine where you are going. This is your carpet, so you can make it go wherever you want it to. Where would you like your carpet to take you?*
- *You can look down if you want, in your mind. What do you see? Where are you going?*
- *Now I'm going to stop talking and I want you to remain on your carpets for 60 seconds, just flying wherever you want, feeling happy and peaceful. Be a silent watcher of yourself.*
- After 60 seconds bring them back by saying, *Now you are going to come back to earth. Let your carpet come down gently, slowly, until you are back in your desk.*

Debrief: Discuss details of your trip with another student.

Extended Debrief: Class discussion leading to literacy assignment.

Showcase: The creation of visuals, stories, descriptions for sharing.

Calm Down

Subject: Any, depending on topic

Individual

5. Imagine This

Objective: To experience the sights, smells, and sounds of an imaginary outing.

- *Sit quietly at your desk, feet on floor, heads on desks.*
- *Close your eyes and breathe deeply.*
- *I am going to take you to an imaginary place. I want you to concentrate on everything you see, hear, smell, and feel. First just concentrate on your breathing—in, out, in, out…*
- *You are lost in the wilderness. (See list below for additional situations.) It is a lovely day, but you are lost.*
- *Look around in your mind. What do you see? What do you hear? What time of day is it? How do you feel?*
- *Walk around slowly. Look at everything. Pay attention to the sounds. Pay attention to the smells. Don't look ahead—look all around you right now.*
- Continue in this manner, focusing on different aspects of sensory awareness depending on the location or theme chosen. The idea is to force students to "be" in this setting and really focus on it in their minds.
- As this motivator is intended to be soothing, keep the images positive. Avoid taking the students' thoughts to negative situations.

Debrief: I strongly encourage debriefing this activity. It can be quick (assuming you want to return to your previous lesson): simply have students share where they were and any dominant images.

Extended Debrief: Since students can experience very strong images, they like to share them with peers or on paper. The images might make ideas for future writing: at this point they can be quickly jotted down in students' writing-idea books; a whole-class discussion could take place prior to a literacy task.

*   *   *

Sample Situations

- In space
- At an old-fashioned farm
- At an amusement park
- On top of a ski hill
- In a plane over the mountains
- At the ocean, on a beautiful beach
- Beside a mountain lake
- In a dark underground cavern
- In the Arctic

- Under the sea
- In a magic kingdom
- On the moon
- Inside a huge tree
- In a meadow filled with flowers
- On a yacht in the middle of a calm sea
- Whitewater rafting in the jungle

6. Time Machine

Objective: To imagine traveling forward or backward in time.

- *Sit quietly at your desks, feet on the floor, heads resting comfortably on your desks.*
- *Breathe deeply; focus on your breathing. Relax completely.*
- *You are very lucky today. You are going to go inside a time machine. Just keep listening to my voice to find out how to do this.*
- *First imagine where you'd like to go. Into the past? To the ages of dinosaurs or cave men? Or into the future? On a rocket ship? On an alien planet?*
- *Take a few breaths to decide silently where you will travel.*
- Wait for about 15 seconds. Then say, *I will count back from ten and, when I get to one, your time machine will whisk you off to your chosen time and place. Get ready—10, 9, 8, 7, 6, 5, 4, 3, 2, 1. Go!*
- Wait for a few seconds, then say, *You are there.*
- *Breathe deeply and take time to look around. What do you see? What do you hear? Smell? Feel? Really pay attention to this time and place. Nothing bad can happen here because you chose a perfect place. Just enjoy it.*
- Wait for about 60 seconds, then say, *When I count up from one to ten, your time machine will start to bring you home again. Here we go—1, 2, 3, 4, 5, 6, 7, 8, 9, 10!*
- *Keep your eyes closed for a few seconds and remember everything you saw and felt.*
- *Now slowly sit up and open your eyes.*

Debrief: I strongly encourage debriefing this activity. It can be quick if you want to return to your previous lesson. Simply have students share with a partner where they were and any dominant images.

Extended Debrief: Since students can experience very strong images, they like to share them with peers or on paper. The images might make ideas for future writing, drama activities, or art projects: ideas could be quickly jotted down in students' writing-idea books; a whole-class discussion could take place prior to a summation task.

Calm Down

Subjects: Any; Health & Wellness
Individual

Note: This refocuser can be done as two separate activities—blasting the bad feeling and then chocolate-covering the good feeling.

7. Chocolate & Bricks

Objective: To release frustrations and replace them with something personal and positive.

- *Sit comfortably, feet on the floor, hands together, eyes closed.*
- *Relax and breathe deeply.*
- *I want you to start to think of something or someone that really annoys you or makes you angry. Now concentrate on the bad feeling—the anger and frustration. Feel it: you are all tense and angry. Feel it in your stomach, in your head—everywhere. I am going to give you 10 seconds to really experience that bad feeling.*
- Wait 10 seconds. *Now take that nasty feeling and cement it inside a solid brick. Push the feeling into the brick. Close the opening with cement. Now you have a heavy, hard brick with the bad feeling inside*
- *Now comes the fun part. In your mind you get to blow up that brick— WAIT until I give you the Blast cue. When I say "Blast," you will imagine blowing up the brick into millions of tiny pieces. The bad feeling will be completely gone.*
- *Get ready—look closely at the brick with your annoying thing inside it. BLAST!*
- *Keep your eyes closed.*
- *Now think of something or someone that makes you very happy. See that thing or person; feel the good feeling; really try to experience the good feeling you get from the thing or person. You feel warm and comfy inside. You are smiling to yourself. I'll give you a few seconds to really feel the good feeling.*
- Wait for about 10 seconds. *Now take the feeling that the good thing gives you and cover it in chocolate. Look at the good feeling all covered in chocolate. What sort of a shape does it make? Can you smell that delicious chocolate?*
- *When I tell you to, in your mind you are going to eat the chocolate. When you do that, the good feeling will stay inside you, making you all warm and tingly.*
- *Ready? Look at the chocolate-covered good feeling. Eat it.*

Extended Debrief: This is an excellent activity to follow with individual journal reflections. Guiding questions might be

- *How did it feel when you blew up the brick?*
- *How did it feel when you ate the chocolate?*
- *Were the feelings different? The same? How? Why?*

Props: Pieces of bubble packing paper (available from any postal outlet)

Prep: Cutting the bubble paper into pieces about the size of students' palms

Notes: A survey found that popping bubble wrap is an authentic stress reliever, as effective as a massage! Why do you think there are so many apps that involve popping bubbles?

8. Pop-a-Lot

Objective: To quickly pop all the bubbles.

- *Sit quietly until I pass out your bubbles. Don't pop any yet.*
- *When I give the Start cue, pop all the bubbles on your section as quickly as you can.*
- *Start!*

Debrief: Discuss what it felt like to pop the bubbles.

Notes
- This is perfect for pre-exam situations.
- Attempt to speak in a slow, quiet, calming monotone for this exercise.

9. Grounding Exercise

Objective: To experience a total sense of calm by using a grounding or centring-of-self technique borrowed from Eastern philosophies.

- *Sit comfortably, feet flat on floor. Don't slouch; sit up straight.*
- *Put your hands together on your desk. Move slightly away from the back of your seat so that you are not leaning against it.*
- *Relax your tongue. Let it lie gently in your mouth. Relax your jaw.*
- *Close your eyes and breathe deeply and quietly—in through your nose, out through your mouth. In—out. In—out…*
- Wait for 10 seconds before continuing: *Now imagine you see a beautiful golden ball floating before you. Look at it—it's swirling and shining and sparkling. So beautiful.*
- *Watch the ball. Really look at in your mind. Keep thinking, "Beautiful golden ball…"*
- Repeat these phrases as many times as needed to allow students to calm down. You will need to use your judgment here, remembering that not all students will have the same experience.
- *Now look closely. The beautiful golden ball is moving toward you—closer, closer. It is moving* inside *you, right into your stomach.*
- *The beautiful golden ball is* in *your stomach* (or *tummy*). *It is making you feel warm, relaxed, wonderful. Feel the ball filling you with golden light, making you calm, confident, relaxed, and happy…*
- *Keep enjoying the feel of the golden ball in your stomach until you hear the Stop cue.*
- Wait for up to 60 seconds then say, *Stop. Let the ball go and open your eyes.*

Debrief: A quick sharing of how it felt is useful here, especially if it's the first time this technique has been used.

Extended Debrief: Excellent to extend to journal reflections. For many students, this technique might be quite surprising and refreshing.

Calm Down

Subjects: Science; Health & Wellness

Individual

10. Hug a Tree

Objective: To experience the sensory imagery of hugging a tree.

- *Sit comfortably at your desk, feet on floor.*
- *Close your eyes and stretch across your desktop.*
- *Spread your arms wide, resting them on the desktop.*
- *Slowly bring your arms together as if hugging a tree.*
- *Stop moving your arms when you get to the size of your tree trunk.*
- *Keep hugging the tree and, in your mind, visualize what your special tree looks like, feels like, smells like.*
- *Keep hugging gently and feel the calm strength of the tree entering you, making you feel relaxed and peaceful. Be very still.*

Calm Down

Subjects: Health & Wellness; Social Studies

Individual

11. Silent Scream

Objective: To demonstrate and release strong emotion using only body language.

- *We all have many strong feelings—emotions. Sometimes we are not able to show them because of where we are or who we are with. We are going to practice some silent emotions.*
- *Sit tall, facing the front, eyes on me. The expressions of emotions are for yourself; it's not necessary to watch other students.*
- *Begin by thinking of being very sad. Think unhappiness and feel it with your body—your eyes, your head, your chest, your hands. Breathe slowly. Very, very sad—feel it and let your body show it for 10 seconds.*
- Take students through each of these emotions: anger, fear, worry, pride, hunger, excitement.
- End with a positive emotion, such as happiness, peacefulness, joy, relaxation, or contentment.

Debrief: A quick review of how it felt to show emotion without words.

Extended Debrief: Journaling about an emotion that is difficult or easy to express silently.

Showcase: Choose who you want to showcase based on what you know about individual students.

Calm Down

Subject: Any
Individual

Notes:

- Similar to Loud Silence on page 148, but with more focus on total body awareness and rigidity.
- A slumped position will contribute to a feeling of relaxation, rather than the feeling of being frozen. The idea is to experience the muscle tension that comes with enforced total stillness.

12. Absolutely Nothing!

Objective: To do absolutely nothing for as long as possible.

- *This is a tough game. You are going to do NOTHING!*
- *Start by sitting comfortably in your chair. Sit tall; do not put your heads on your desks and do not slouch. Think tall and straight!*
- *When I give the Start cue, you are going to freeze—not move at all, not make a single sound—for a full minute. Sounds easy doesn't it? It's not.*
- *Check to see if you are comfy and firmly rooted to your chair, with no body parts hanging over, and in a position you can hold without moving—not even to scratch!*
- *Try to still your diaphragm; breathe slowly and very quietly.*
- *You are a statue! Even your mind is still. Begin.*
- Work up to 60 seconds (and more). It's difficult for students to remain motionless and silent for this amount of time.

Debrief: Discuss what was difficult/easy about the game.

Extended Debrief: Challenge students to think of situations in which total immobility and silence might be necessary.

Calm Down

Subject: Language Arts
Individual

13. The Key

Objective: To creatively imagine what could be done with a mysterious key.

- *Sit comfortably. You can put your heads on your desks if you want to.*
- *Close your eyes and breathe deeply. Listen to my voice.*
- *I want you to visualize—see in your mind—a huge, very old key. Look at it. What shape is it? What color? Think only about that amazing key.*
- *Now you see five or six doors in front of you.*
- *Think of a door to open with your key. Imagine what you might see/smell/feel/hear when the key opens one of the doors.*
- Wait for about 20 seconds: *Now go to the door you chose. Use your magic key to open it and take yourself on a magical journey.*
- Wait about 20 seconds. *See, hear, smell, and even taste everything behind your magical door. Pay attention to and memorize details of color, texture, odor. Stay in your magical place until I give you the Stop cue.*
- Watch for restlessness and time the activity accordingly. Usually students can remain in the process comfortably for up to two minutes.

Extended Debrief: An excellent pre-writing activity, if discussion occurs between the guided imagery and the writing process. Leading questions include

- *What did your key look/feel/smell like?*
- *What did the doors look like? Why did you choose the one you chose?*
- *Did the key stick in the door or open easily?*
- *What was the first thing you noticed when the door opened?*
- *Did you go through the door? Why or why not?*
- *Describe your magical journey. How did you feel while you were on it?*

14. Lift Off!

Objective: To imagine the body levitating or lifting out of the desk into the air.

- *Sit comfortably in your desk, feet flat on the floor. Rest your head on your arms and close your eyes.*
- *Breathe deeply in through your nose, out through your mouth.*
- *Be silent and listen to my voice.*
- *You feel very heavy, like a solid rock. Heavy, heavy… Think of pressure pushing down on you—pushing hard, making you heavier and heavier.*
- *Keep thinking of the pressure and the heaviness of your body—your legs, your arms, your head…*
- Wait for about 20 seconds before continuing: *Now something magical is happening. Suddenly you feel the pressure being lifted off.*
- *Your feet and legs start to feel light. They almost lift right off the floor.*
- *Your body feels lighter and lighter.*
- *The light feeling moves into your shoulders, head, arms…lighter, lighter…*
- *You are so light you start to feel yourself lift right off the chair—in your mind, not in reality.*
- *Now imagine you are actually lifting up, rising up into the air—slowly, like a weightless bubble. Lifting, rising up, up, up… Lighter and lighter…*
- Continue coaching in this way for as long as you feel is appropriate, then cue with, *You will gently float around until you hear the Stop cue.*

Debrief: *What did it feel like?* Encourage sharing between students for a few seconds before returning to the interrupted lesson.

Calm Down

Subjects: Health & Wellness; Language Arts; Math; Science

Individual

Note: This is similar to Lift Off (above) but is quicker and easier to execute.

15. Featherweight Arms

Objective: To experience the feeling of arms floating or rising on their own.

- *Sit with your feet flat on the floor and your hands and forearms flat on your desktop. This is sometimes called the Sphinx position.*
- *When I give the Start cue, you will push down on the desktop with your hands and arms as hard as you can, without standing up.*
- Give the Start cue and verbally encourage students to push hard for 30 seconds. This is harder than it seems.
- Provide the Stop cue and immediately say, *Allow your arms to float up. Notice how they seem weightless. Just let them float and enjoy the feeling.*
- Allow students to experience the feeling of weightlessness in their arms for about 30 seconds, then debrief.

Debrief: *Think about the way your arms felt when you first stopped pushing. How can you describe that? Why do you think it happened?*

Calm Down

Subject: Science

Individual

Note: This activity can be done while seated, but is more effective on the floor.

16. Catitude

Objective: To mimic the relaxing actions of a stretching cat.

- *For this activity you will start on your hands and knees beside your desk.*
- *Listen quietly and follow my directions.*
- *You are a cat—a silent cat. You have just woken from a long, relaxing nap and are going to stretch.*
- *First, flex your back downward, dropping your stomach close to the floor and stretching your neck up.*
- *Now do the opposite; curl your back high like a Halloween cat.*
- *Repeat these two actions once more.*
- *Stretch your front right paw as far forward as possible…slowly, slowly. Then reach forward with your other front paw.*
- *Remember—you are stretching and relaxing, stretching and relaxing.*
- *Curl up into a tiny ball and stay like that, feeling very warm and relaxed, until I cue you to return to your seats.*
- Allow about 30 seconds in this position.

Calm Down

Subject: Science

Individual

17. Telescope

Objective: To imagine looking at an object through a very powerful telescope.

- *Sit comfortably with your feet on the floor and your head on your arms. Close your eyes.*
- *If you prefer to sit up straight and close your eyes, that's okay too.*
- *You are very comfortable.*
- *Breathe deeply in through your nose, out through your mouth.*
- *Imagine you have in front of you a very powerful telescope. This telescope will allow you to see in great detail anything you want to see. For example, you might want to look at your own hand and see all the tiny lines, colors, wrinkles…whatever. Or you might want to look at something far away, like the moon. You could see all the details of the surface of the moon.*
- *Think for a few seconds about what it is you'll examine through your telescope. Don't look through your telescope yet. Just think of what you will look at. I'll tell you when to look through the telescope.*
- Wait for about 20 seconds, then cue students to begin looking. Side coach for a few seconds, then remain quiet for up to two minutes.

Debrief: Invite students to share what they were examining. This should be a very quick once-around-the-room sharing.

Extended Debrief: Write or discuss the detailed images.

Calm Down

Subject: Language Arts

Individual

Props: A jar or bag of simple, age-appropriate jokes, collected and written on individual slips of paper

Prep: This does take some teacher planning ahead of time, but is well worth the effort. There are many joke sites online. Collecting and selecting jokes could be a job for an aid or volunteer.

18. Joke in a Jar

Objective: To listen to and enjoy a randomly chosen joke.

- *Sit comfortably and watch me. We will all have a laugh together…or maybe a groaner.*
- *If it's a good joke, we'll indicate by a thumbs-up at the end. If it's a groaner, we'll give a thumbs-down. Remember, not everyone will feel the same way and there is no right or wrong response.*
- Pick a joke and share.
- Wait for about 5 seconds before calling, *Thumbs, please.*
- Share one to three jokes—no more.

Debrief: *What made this joke funny/not funny?*

Calm Down

Subjects: Health & Wellness; Language Arts; Science; Social Studies

Individual

Props: A collection of interesting school facts, collected and written on individual slips of paper

Prep: Like Joke in a Jar, this activity calls for teacher preparation in the collection of interesting school facts. Collecting and selecting facts could be a job for an aid or volunteer.

Notes:
- Collecting and selecting facts could be done by a class that is mentoring your own.
- This activity can be easily transformed into a trivia challenge. Students of all ages enjoy trivia!

19. Fun School Facts

Objective: To enjoy interesting facts about your school.

- *Sit quietly and listen carefully.*
- *You are going to be amazed by some facts about our school*
- Read a few facts, or select students to read them.

Debrief: *Which fact surprised you the most? Why?*

* * *

Suggestions for Fun School Facts

- When the school was built.
- How many students/teachers/support staff there are.
- Changes that have been made to the facility/curriculum/surrounding area.
- School rules that have changed/developed.
- The first principal.
- The current principal's middle name.
- Specific fun facts about teachers; don't forget to get teachers' approval first. Examples include
  - *Who just had an anniversary/birthday/baby/grandbaby.*
  - *Who has been to Hawaii/Mexico/Russia/etc.*
  - *Who plays basketball/hockey.*
  - *Who skis/dances/sings/swims/competes in…/etc.*

Calm Down

Subjects: Art; Health & Wellness; Science

Individual as part of a group

Props: Bubble mixture, bought or made ahead of time

Prep: You can mix 1 part glycerin, 1 part liquid dish detergent, and 1 part water. Keep bubble mixture in a closed container. This makes big, beautiful bubbles. Twist a piece of wire into a closed hoop or use any item that will hold a film of the mixture.

20. Bubble Brigade

Objective: To watch bubbles float and to concentrate on their beauty.

- *Sit quietly and watch what I am about to do.*
- Blow a few bubbles.
- *Now look even closer and see if you can see any colors or unusual shapes.*
- Blow more bubbles.
- *Gently blow on any bubble that comes near you to try to keep it in the air as long as possible.*
- Continue for about two minutes. Insist that students remain seated throughout. Walk around while blowing the bubbles so that all students get the experience of gently blowing the bubbles away.

Pencil and Paper

Useful at any time when students simply need a break, Pencil and Paper activities are especially effective following a more physical class, such as a movement, Phys Ed, or Fine Arts class. In these instances they serve as a transition from a big activity to a smaller or more focused seatwork activity.

The motivators in this section continue to keep students at their desks, but differ from Calm Down activities in that they require more active, often more stimulating, involvement. Because students are expected to react quickly using paper and writing tools, these tasks tend to be more cognitive and arousing. Many of them are competitive in nature, encouraging quick thinking (Scrabble Scramble, page 48), careful predictions (Never-ending Line, page 42), or directed concentration (Written Rumor, page 45). Students love these motivators, probably because they encourage creativity in a context where no response is incorrect. They work well before lessons requiring careful penmanship (Zoom Out, page 47), fine motor control (Mirror Images, page 49), active listening (Draw My Words, page 43), or literary concepts (Letter Scramble, page 41).

Unlike the Calm Down activities for individual students, most of these motivators involve working in partners or small groups, so socialization and communication are also addressed. However, most of them are silent activities; no-talking rules will have to be reinforced. Remind students of the power of nonverbal communication.

A few of the refocusers require some teacher preparation in the form of accumulation of words/facts (e.g., Word Lotto, page 41) but this can be done on-the-spot if necessary.

Teachers will have their own favorite ways to pair students, but a little advanced thought as to which method will be used will prevent possible arguments and classroom disruption:

- Often the quickest way to have students pair off is to simply have them partner with an adjacent peer: *Turn to the person behind/beside you...*
- Another quick way to pair students is to have them count numbers in sequence: 1 and 2 are partners, 3 and 4, and so on.
- It is always a good idea to change the partnering system regularly to encourage new relationships and provide opportunities for many chances for students to learn from others.

Pencil and Paper

Subjects: Art; Health & Wellness; Science

Individual

Props: One piece of scrap paper per student, any size (it can have text or be blank); individual writing tools

Note: Scribbling, as well as crumpling and tearing paper, provides relief from frustration or anxiety, and encourage endorphins to flow. They also reduce nervous energy by giving it a healthy outlet.

21. Scribble, Crumple & Tear

Objective: To scribble on a page, crumple it, tear it into small pieces, and dispose of it.

- *Choose a tool for writing. It can be anything you like.*
- *When I give the Start cue, scribble all over the paper. Try to fill your scribbles with feelings. Are you angry? Bored? Frustrated? Show that in your scribbles.*
- Cue to start and allow 30 seconds of scribbling.
- Cue to stop.
- *Crumple your page up into a tiny ball. Use lots of* quiet *energy.*
- *Now open your page and tear it into tiny, tiny pieces. Again, use* quiet *energy.*
- Allow 60–90 seconds for the crushing and tearing.

Debrief: Discuss how it felt to destroy the paper. Ask what, if any, feelings students experienced during the refocuser and invite suggestions as to how/when they could use this activity on their own.

Pencil and Paper

Subjects: Art; Health & Wellness

Individual

Props: One piece of paper per student; individual writing tools

22. Zen Garden

Objective: To trace curved lines with your fingers.

- Hand out pieces of paper, or have students use their own.
- *When I give the Start cue, you will fill your paper with gently waving lines, going from the top of the page to the bottom.*
- *You will begin by drawing a single line like this.* Model a curvy line on the board or on your own paper. Avoid making it complicated; it should be a gentle curve such as might be seen in a Zen garden or a sandy beach.
- *Fill the page by drawing other lines close to, but not touching, the first line. Leave a space of ½ cm (¼ inch) between the lines. Every line will follow the first line until your page is filled.*
- *When you are finished, put your pen down and sit quietly.*
- Allow about 30 seconds for this, or until students are finished. Side coach as necessary.
- *When I give the Start cue, use your fingers to slowly follow the curved lines from top to bottom, over and over again. Focus on the gentle curves. Trace softly, gently, with your fingers barely touching the paper.*
- *Keep doing this until I give the Stop cue.*

Debrief: Quickly discuss how it felt to carry out this task. Most students find it extremely calming.

Extended Debrief: Learn about Zen gardens by doing an Internet search.

Pencil and Paper

Subjects: Language Arts; Health & Wellness

Individual

Props: One piece of lined paper per student; individual writing tools

Note: This is a great anticipatory set for a writing task based on memory. It might seem very rushed, but sometimes the best memories are the ones most easily and quickly accessed.

23. One-Minute Memory

Objective: To quickly recall and jot down a single memory.

- Hand out paper. Have students choose a writing tool.
- *Sit comfortably with paper and writing tool in front of you.*
- *When I give the Start cue, shut your eyes and think for a few seconds about a memory—any memory. It an be anything you remember doing or seeing or thinking or hearing…*
- *I will allow you 30 seconds for you to think of the memory.*
- *When I give the Start cue again, jot down the most important words or points about that memory. You will have only two minutes to write.*
- Cue to begin the thinking.
- Cue to begin the writing.

Debrief: Invite one or two students to share what they wrote, or ask students to save the jot notes for a future task.

Pencil and Paper

Subject: Any

Partners

Props: One piece of paper per partnership; individual writing tools

24. Box Me In

Objective: To avoid being boxed-in in a simple game of chance and cognition.

- *Partners should sit as close together as possible. You might have to move a chair and use one desk between you for this game.*
- *You each need something to write with; you need one piece of paper between you.*
- *Put four dots across the page about 2.5 cm or 1 inch apart, then put four dots going down, then fill in the square with spaced dots. You will have 16 dots all together.* Model on board: a 4-by-4 square made up of dots.
- *Here's the game. Decide which partner will start.* Wait until they decide.
- *Starter connects any two dots to make a straight line. Then the other person connects any two dots, and so on.*
- *Here's the trick. The boxes represent little jails. You want to stay out of them. That means you do NOT want to be forced to draw the last line that completes a box. If you do, you must put your initial in that box—go to jail—and take another turn.*
- *The person with the LEAST number of initials in boxes is the winner, because he/she has been to jail the least number of times.*
- *Remember that this is a silent activity.*

Pencil and Paper

Subjects: Science; Math

Partners

Props: One piece of paper per partnership; individual writing tools

Note: Students will be tempted to talk. Remind them that no oral communication is allowed.

25. Circles & Squares

Objective: To create, with a partner but using no oral communication, an interesting illustration or abstract picture using only circles and squares.

- *Decide between you who will be the Circle and who will be the Square.*
- *You and your partner will have two minutes to create an interesting picture. But here's the catch—you can use only your designated shape. Squares partners can draw only squares and Circles partners can draw only circles.*
- *And…you can't talk to each other. You just have to start drawing—taking turns—and see what happens.*
- Cue to start.
- Warn students when there are only 30 seconds left.
- Cue to stop.
- *You now have 30 seconds to discuss with your partner what your drawing could be. Maybe it's abstract. Decide now.*
- Stop them after 30 seconds.

Debrief: Quickly allow each pair to show and name their drawing.

Pencil and Paper

Subject: Any

Partners

Props: One piece of paper per partnership; individual writing tools

26. O's and X's

Objective: To play a paper and pencil game, the opposite to the familiar X's and O's.

- *This game is like the game you know as X's and O's, but it's just the opposite.*
- *Start by drawing two vertical lines with two horizontal lines through them.* Model the grid.
- *You now have nine empty boxes.*
- *Decide who is X and who is O.*
- *Take turns putting your signs in boxes. Your job is to avoid making a straight line with your sign. If your partner forces you to make a straight line, you're out.*
- *Remember there is no talking. If someone is out before I give the Sstop cue, start again.*

Pencil and Paper

Subjects: Art; Math; Science
Partners

Props: One piece of paper per partnership; individual writing tools

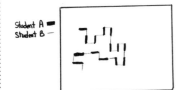

27. Two-Centimetre Trail

Objective: To draw two-centimetre lines at right angles to each other

- *You and your partner will have one sheet of paper between you.*
- *Your job is to make little lines, about 2 centimetres (1 inch) in length. You might want to review this length.*
- *Every line must connect to the previous line at a right angle, or 90 degrees. No line can cross over another line. Demonstrate with a few lines.*
- *You need to work as a team so you don't get boxed in or stuck at one side of the page, unable to move any further. You must think ahead, but you cannot talk to each other while you are doing it.*
- *Keep going until I cue you to stop. Then we'll compare pages.*

Showcase: A good activity to display under a heading such as *Cooperation*.

Pencil and Paper

Subject: Language Arts
Partners

Props: One piece of paper and one writing tool per student

28. Letter Scramble

Objective: To randomly write five letters, then add them to a partner's five letters to make words.

- *When I give the Start cue, write five letters on your page. Don't let your partner see what you're writing.*
- *On either of your pieces of paper, put together the letters you have both written, and make as many words from these letters as possible.*
- *If you both have chosen the same letter, that means you can use that letter twice in a word. Otherwise, each letter can only be used once in a word.*
- *You will have two minutes. Go!*
- At the end of two minutes, check for winning pairs. Do a quick check for accuracy. Point out that a lot depended on which letters they initially chose. Once students have played this game a few times, they become expert at selecting the letters that can be included in the maximum number of words.

Pencil and Paper

Subject: Any as source of words
Partners

Props: One piece of paper and one writing tool per partnership

Prep: Compile a list of 10–15 (or 20–25) words; they can be random or subject-related, wordwall–related, spelling-related, etc. Transpose the words onto slips of paper.

29. Word Lotto

Objective: To randomly select words with a partner, and take a chance that they will be the words chosen by the teacher.

- *Make a large + on your page, made of two lines intersecting. Or Make a grid of two vertical and two horizontal lines.*
- *From our list of words, choose any four and write one in each square. Or Choose nine words and write one word in each square.*
- *I will randomly draw a word from the list. If you have that word, draw a line or an X through it.*
- *The first pair to have lines through all their words wins.*

Pencil and Paper

Subject: Any

Individual

Props: One piece of paper and one writing tool per student

Note: Drawing a diagram and writing a few words about thinking provides a reminder of how we think, and can serve as a future reference for tough thinking tasks.

30. Thinking Cap

Objective: To draw and write about an imaginary thinking cap.

- *Thinking is important. We all do it all the time. But sometimes thinking is harder than at other times, and that's when you might have heard the expression "Put on your thinking cap."*
- *You get to have some fun imagining what your own private thinking cap might look like, and then drawing it.*
- *Be creative. Be silly if you want to, but draw that cap. You have one minute.* Wait for about 60 seconds.
- *Close your eyes and imagine you are putting that cap on.* Wait for 20 seconds.
- *Pay attention to how you are feeling with that thinking cap on. Choose two or three words that describe how you are feeling.*
- *When I cue you, open your eyes and write those words beside your cap.*
- Cue to open eyes and write.

Debrief: Students can share their diagrams and words with others or can develop this further into a writing or creating task.

Pencil and Paper

Subjects: Art; Math; Science

Partners

Props: One piece of unlined paper and one writing tool per partnership

31. Never-ending Line

Objective: To draw a picture with a partner, sharing a single pencil and using a non-stopping line.

- *Each pair of you should have one sheet of paper and one writing tool.*
- *You and your partner are to create an interesting picture—but there's a catch. Once you put the pencil on the paper, you cannot lift the pencil again until I give the Stop cue. Your picture will be made from one continuous, never-ending line, and you'll take turns making it.*
- *You cannot speak to each other. You have to try to read your partner's mind to figure out what he or she is trying to draw. No nonverbal communication, such as drawing in the air or hand signals, either.*
- *Every time you hear my cue, the writing tool moves to the other partner. The person receiving the writing tool picks up where the partner stopped and keeps going.*
- *Remember, you can't discuss what you are drawing. It just has to grow out of the line you are making.*
- Model or give an example using students' names: e.g., *I am Brenda and I draw this line. Then the cue comes and I hand the pencil to Sandy who adds to it like this…*
- Cue to start. Cue about every five seconds, for up to about two minutes.
- *Now you and your partner have 20 seconds to decide what your picture is. Then we'll quickly share.*

Debrief: Invite each pair to hold up their drawing and tell what it is.

Extended Debrief: Discuss how drawing this way can be compared to rumors growing from nothing. Discuss also how sometimes we have to make educated guesses as to what another person means, and what clues and cues there might be to help us.

Pencil and Paper

Subjects: Art; Science; Language Arts

Partners

Props: One piece of paper and one writing tool per partnership; a picture (optional)

32. Draw My Words

Objective: To "copy" an illustration by listening to a partner's directions.

- *Decide who will be the Speaker and who will be the Artist.*
- *All Artists now turn away from the front of the room.* (If you are using an overhead or the interactive whiteboard, you don't want them to see the illustration or word.)
- Make an illustration (best with younger students) or word clearly visible to the Speakers. Picture props (illustrations of simple objects) or simple items, such as keys, a pair of glasses, or coffee mug, can be used, or students can draw from spoken directions.
- *Speakers, your job is to get your partner to reproduce/draw this illustration/word/item by giving them verbal cues only. But you can't tell them exactly what they are drawing. The only directions you can provide are words for shapes, lines, or placement on the page. For example, you might say, "At the top of the page draw a circle."*
- *You have two minutes to talk your partner through the entire drawing.*
- Cue to start and stop. Circulate to watch for students giving too much information or too-specific hints.
- You might choose to have students trade off, so that Speakers become Drawers and vice versa. As this takes longer, it could become your choice the next time 3-Minute Motivator is required.

Showcase: Invite sharing of diagrams.

*   *   *

Sample Illustrations

- Fish, mermaids, octopuses, whales, jellyfish, starfish
- Animals, such as rabbits, cats, dogs, elephants, giraffes, turtles
- Cars, trucks, trains, boats
- Stick people "in action"
- Flowers, trees, birds, butterflies, ladybugs
- House, barn, church, teepee, tent, hut

Sample In-class Items

- Cups, glasses, containers
- Hats, reading glasses, clothing items, pieces of jewelry
- Writing tools, scissors, stapler

Pencil and Paper

Subject: Math

Partners

Props: Two pieces of paper per partnership; individual writing tools

Note: This is a great math practice game; difficulty that can be increased or decreased by changing the size of the original numbers and the type of operation. It can be used successfully even with fractions and decimals.

33. Number Madness

Objective: To use previously chosen numbers to arrive at teacher-provided numerals.

- *Divide one of your pages into four by making a big + in the middle. In each quadrant, put any number between 0 and 9.*
- *The other page is for keeping score. Don't write on it yet.*
- *I will say a number. If you have that number written on your page, give yourself a point on the score page.* Demonstrate if necessary.
- *If you can* make *that number, by adding/subtracting/dividing multiplying* (Decide which operation to use depending on student abilities; provide only one operation at a time), *then give yourself two points. You and your partner can quickly discuss this possibility.*

  For example, the number called is 4 and the operation is Addition. If I have the number 4 in a quadrant, I get a point for it. If I also have the numbers 1 and 3 on my page, then I can add 1 and 3 to get 4, for two points. That would mean I got a total of 3 points when the number 4 is called.

- *If you use two or more numbers to get the called number, write the operation and the numbers on the score sheet; e.g., 1 + 3 = 4.*
- *At the end of the game, quickly add up your points; I can check to see if your operations are done correctly.*

Sample Number Square and Scoring

$$1 + 3 + 7 = 11 \qquad\qquad 3 + 1 = 4$$

$$\Large 1 \qquad\qquad 3$$

$$4 + 3 = 7 \qquad\qquad 7 + 4 = 11$$

$$\Large 4 \qquad\qquad 7$$

Scoring

Using addition

Number called	Points
4	3 (1 point for number in quadrant; 2 points from 3 + 1)
9	0
3	1
11	4 (2 points from 1 + 3 + 7; 2 points from 7 + 4)

Pencil and Paper

Subject: Language Arts
Small Group (5–6)

Props: One sheet of paper (preferably lined) per group; individual writing tools

34. Written Rumor

Objective: To write and rewrite a statement, and to observe the changes.

- *In this game, every person reads the sentence written on the paper by the person before him or her, then hides that sentence from view by folding the paper.* Model how to fold paper horizontally to cover the previous sentence.
- *Then he or she rewrites the sentence so that it means the same thing—or almost the same thing—but using different words. For example, if the sentence says, "I went to town to buy groceries," I could write, "I went to the store to buy bread and milk."*
- *Each person will have just a few seconds to silently read, rewrite, and pass the paper on.*
- *This is a timed game. At the end of 60 seconds, we will share what each group has written.*
- *Remember, no talking.*
- *I will give you the sentence to start, but only the first person in the group can see it. Everyone else, please put your heads down and close your eyes. The first person in each group has to write the sentence on your group's piece of paper.*
- Write a sentence on the board or interactive whiteboard; see suggestions below. Then allow all students to sit up and get ready for their turns.

Debrief: Share the final writings. Quickly discuss how they have changed and why.

Extended Debrief: This activity lends itself to in-depth discussions of how and why rumors start, gather speed, get corrupted, etc.

*   *   *

Sample Opening Sentences

- The animals in the jungle were in danger of extinction.
- The students ran from the school when the fire alarm went off.
- In my kitchen there are cooking utensils and food.
- My backpack is a thing of wonder because it holds so many precious items.
- The movie was scary but the popcorn was buttery and good.
- All the kids in our class have good work skills, good manners, and good hairstyles.
- I have a perfect pet because it is small and cuddly.
- My favorite teacher is smart, cares, and has a great sense of humor.
- It is my plan to become rich and famous without having to work too hard.

Pencil and Paper

Subject: Language Arts

Partners

Props: One piece of paper and one writing tool per partnership

35. Shared-Pen Stories

Objective: To cooperatively write a sentence or short story with a single writing tool.

- Pair students and provide a single piece of blank paper per pair; consider pairing heterogeneously (not always "the person next to you").
- *You are going to write a story (sentence) together, but you cannot talk about what you are going to write.*
- *I will give you a topic, then partner A will start writing whatever comes to mind.*
- *When I give the cue, partner B will take the writing tool and continue on from where A left off. Partner B doesn't know exactly what A had in mind, but does know the general topic, and must stick to that topic.*
- *Remember—no talking. You just have to guess what your partner might have been going to write.*
- *When you think a thought is finished, put a period after it and continue writing until the cue to hand off the writing tool.*
- Cue approximately every ten seconds. This might need to be adjusted according to students' age.
- *When I tell you to stop, you will read over what you have written together. See if it makes sense—and be prepared to share.*

Debrief: Encourage sharing of sentences/stories with other pairs or the whole class. Discuss the difficulties in figuring out what each partner was thinking. Discuss how/where/when a situation like this could happen in daily life.

* * *

Sample Topics

- pet peeves
- homework
- sisters or brothers
- friends
- dreams, fears, worries
- best adventure ever
- *When I grow up…*
- favorite foods

Pencil and Paper

Subject: Language Arts; Health & Wellness

Partners

Props: One piece of paper and one writing tool per student

36. Teddy Bear or Tiger

Objective: To examine personal behavior(s) and share with a partner.

- *We all have two different sides to us: sometimes we are teddy bears; sometimes we are tigers. For example, I am a teddy bear when I have to meet new people, because I'm sort of timid; and I am a tiger when I stand up for my students.*
- *Please write* Teddy Bear *on one side of your paper and* Tiger *on the other.*
- *When I give the Start cue, you will have one minute to think of an example of how/why/when you fit into both categories.*
- Cue and watch. You might need to allow more time if students are slow.
- *Now turn to your partner and share what you've written.*

Debrief: Invite any students who feel comfortable enough doing so to share with the class. Save these pages for further discussion and writing tasks.

Pencil and Paper

Subject: Science

Partners

Props: One piece of paper per partnership; individual writing tools

Notes:
- An excellent resource for this type of thinking is the picture book *Zoom* by Istvan Banyai.
- Quiet conversation is allowed during this refocuser.

37. Zoom Out

Objective: To create a picture/illustration that begins with a very tiny detail and works outward.

- *Your job will be to create something that naturally starts very small and gets gradually larger. For example, like looking first at your fingernail, then gradually expanding the focus to your whole body.*
- *For this activity there can be quiet talking as you and your partner figure out what you are drawing. It might take a few moments for you to do this.*
- *In the meantime, keep adding to the picture. Maybe it will end up being an abstract or design, and that's okay too.*
- *Partner A, please draw a dot in the centre of the page.*
- *Now Partner B, without discussion, add something to the dot. Keep it small.*
- *Each time I cue, you will hand over the paper, taking turns adding something to the drawing, moving from the centre of the page outward.*
- Cue every ten seconds or so. If students are stuck, make suggestions, such as *Maybe it could be an eye, a spot on something, a button, a pimple.* Once students get the idea, this task truly catapults.

Debrief: Discuss how capable students were of creating an actual representation of something. Invite them to name their illustrations.

Extended Debrief: Discuss where in science we try to look closely at objects or beings like this. Discuss/write about this concept.

Showcase: Encourage sharing the finished, labeled illustrations and even posting them for others to enjoy.

Pencil and Paper

Subjects: Language Arts; Health & Wellness

Individual

Props: Writing tools, paper

38. My Up, My Down

Objective: To list some personal positives and not-so-positives

- *We all have qualities that we like and dislike about ourselves. For example I like that I… and I dislike that I… Share qualities about yourself.*
- *Draw a line down the middle of your page from top to bottom. On one side at the top put a plus sign (+); on the other side at the top put a minus sign (-).*
- *When I give the Start cue, jot down things about yourself that you think are good (plus) and not-so-good (minus). Put them under the correct sign.*
- *It doesn't matter if there are more points on one side than the other.*
- *No one will read this except you.*
- Give the Start cue. After three minutes, give the Stop cue and have students turn their pages face-down. Privacy is important for this task.
- This 3-Minute Motivator can end with the lists, as creating them is both cathartic and stress reducing, or you can have student save lists for future writing tasks.

Debrief: Discuss what might have been difficult about this task.

Extended Debrief: Create a writing assignment based on the lists.

Pencil and Paper

Subjects: Language Arts; Any as source of theme

Partners

Props: One piece grid paper per partnership; individual writing tools

Prep: Compile lists of theme-based words; e.g. words relating to current science studies

39. Scrabble Scramble

Objective: To create a crossword puzzle using words related to a theme.

- Give each pair of students a sheet of paper with a grid, such as graph paper; the squares should be sized according to the age/ability of your students.
- *This activity involves you being creative with words and putting them together to form a crossword puzzle—just like playing Scrabble. You can use the squares on the sheet or make them as big as you need to.*
- *I will give you the list of words to use. You and your partner pick any one you want to begin with, then try to fit in as many of the others as you can.*
- *With the exception of three* freebies, *use only these words. Freebies are any words at all that fit, and that might make it easier for you to get more theme words into your puzzle. Remember, you have only three freebies.*
- *You will have two minutes* (or more, depending on your purpose) *to see who can fit the most words together.*

Debrief: Survey to see how many words were correctly used. Select winners. If there is a tie, the partnership using the fewest freebies wins.

Extended Debrief: Make further use of the created puzzles by having students write definitions in appropriate crossword style; i.e., lists of Across and Down clues. They can then exchange with other pairs to complete the blank crosswords.

Pencil and Paper

Subjects: Health & Wellness; Language Arts; Social Studies (theme of haves and have-nots)

Individual

Props: Blindfolds; one piece of paper and one writing tool per student

Notes:
- Simple blindfolds can be made from an old sheet torn into strips. Once you have a class set of blindfolds, it's amazing how many uses you'll find for them.
- Instead of blindfolds, you can have students close their eyes—but can you really trust them not to peek?

40. Blind Draw

Objective: To try to draw (or write) without looking.

- *For this game you will work alone. In fact, you will be more alone than usual, as you will be blindfolded.*
- *You job will be to write (or draw) without looking at your page, beginning and stopping on cue.*
- *Start by feeling the edges of your page before you put on your blindfold (or close your eyes).*
- *Get ready—blindfolds on. Don't peek; it will be much more fun if you follow this rule. You will remain seated at your desk and totally safe.*
- *I will tell you what to write (or draw).*
- *Ready? Begin. Keep writing (or drawing) until I give the Stop cue.*
- After about two minutes, give the Stop cue.
- *Uncover your eyes and look at your work. How good is it? You may share it with a neighbor. Why was that difficult?*

Debrief: You can tie this activity to lessons about differentiation, handicaps, or even the concept of some having less than others in our society or in the world in general.

Pencil and Paper

Subject: Any

Partners

Props: One sheet of paper and one writing tool per partnership

Note: Having a snowglobe as a visual cue adds greatly to this refocuser.

41. Snowglobe Drawings

Objective: To connect random dots into a reasonable facsimile of a picture.

- *Pair up and decide who's A and who's B.*
- *Partner B, think of a snowglobe. Pretend you are inside one and draw the snowflakes all over your page by filling the page with dots. But remember to make them scattered like snowflakes; they are not sheets of rain.*
- *I am going to put a limit on the number of snowflakes in your globe.* Tell them a number from 20 to 40. Use fewer dots for younger students: the more dots there are, the more difficult the task.
- *Okay, begin. Partner B, make your dots anywhere you want on the page.*
- *Now it's A's turn. Partner A, you must find a way to connect these dots to make a picture. And you have to use all the dots on the page. Your picture might have to be an abstract. You have one minute to do this.*
- Have students switch roles so both have a chance to try each part of this creative activity. Students are much more adept at joining random dots than adults are, and you might be surprised at the results.

Debrief: *You may take a few moments to talk about your pictures with other students.* Encourage quiet conversation for no more than 30 seconds.

Extended Debrief: This could lead to a Language Arts writing assignment on snow: e.g., a story about a snowstorm, a graphic description of a snowstorm, an essay about snow safety.

Pencil and Paper

Subjects: Language Arts; Math; Science

Partners

Props: One piece of paper and one writing tool per partnership

Notes:
- Since most children are right-handed, and since making the mirror image is more difficult than creating the first illustration, allow the mirrors to use the right side of the page. After the initial copying, alternating to add small details is less difficult.
- A more-difficult alternative is to have the student using the left side of the paper use his or her left hand to draw.

42. Mirror Images

Objective: To create symmetrical illustrations or designs.

- *Everyone has looked in a mirror. When you do this, the image you see is actually the opposite of yourself. For each pair, one of you will be the mirror.*
- *Begin by folding your paper lengthwise to make a crease, then opening it flat again.*
- *Decide who's A and who's B. Partner A, you will work on the LEFT side of the crease; B will work on the RIGHT.*
- *Partner A, begin by drawing a simple thing—an object, such as an apple or a flower. (It might be easier for some students to start with single lines—a curved line, a diagonal line—before moving to shapes).*
- *Partner B, try to reproduce a symmetrical mirror image, the way the picture would look in a mirror.*
- *Partner B, add something to the image for Partner A to copy on the left side.*
- *Continue in this manner until I cue you to stop.*

Debrief: *Look closely at your pages. Is one side exactly symmetrical with the other? How can you check?* (Refold the crease and hold up to the light to see if the lines correspond.)

Extended Debrief: You might wish to discuss problems with this task, or where, in nature or real life, symmetry exists.

Pencil and Paper

Subjects: Language Arts; ; Math; Science

Partners

Props: One piece of paper and one writing tool per partnership

43. Air Writing

Objective: To write a sentence or series of words on paper, after seeing it written in the air.

- *In partners, decide who is A and who is B.*
- *Partner A, turn your back to your partner. Write a simple sentence in the air in front of you, one word at a time, allowing time for your partner to write the same sentence on paper.*
- Encourage cursive writing if that is the stage your students are at. Suggest the form as well as the approximate number of words in the sentence.
- *Remember you are a team; you are not trying to confuse your partner. You want him/her to be able to copy your message correctly.*
- After 60–90 seconds, have students switch roles so that each partner has a chance to copy the air writing.

Debrief: Discuss what was difficult or easy about this task, as well as where/when in life such a situation might occur; e.g., sending a message to someone who is too far away to hear you.

Pencil and Paper

Subjects: History (hieroglyphics); Language Arts; Science; Social Studies

Partners

Props: One piece of paper and one writing tool per partnership

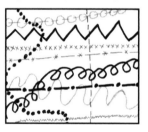

Student A —
Student B —

44. Line Challenge

Objective: To create as many different forms/types of lines as you can in 60 seconds.

- *You and your partner will take turns drawing lines—just lines—across the page.*
- *Your challenge is to think of and draw as many different kinds of lines as you can—thin lines, squiggly lines, fuzzy lines, and so on.*
- *You cannot repeat a line that your partner has drawn, so each partner has to create a different-looking line every turn.*
- *The lines can cross each other and go anywhere you want them to on the page.*
- *Don't just scribble. THINK about the lines.*
- *You will start when I give the Start cue and stop when I give the Stop cue.*
- Allow no more than 90 seconds between the Start and Stop cues.

Debrief: Allow students to share their pages and indicate their favorite lines. Discuss where and when variety in lines might be seen/used.

Pencil and Paper

Subjects: Art; Language Arts

Partners

Props: One sheet of paper and one writing tool per partnership

Note: Young children initially draw people as stick figures. As it allows students to play with a constantly moving line to create a figure just like they used to do, this refocuser is rewarding and easy.

45. Scribble People

Objective: To draw interacting figures of people made entirely out of scribbles.

- *I want to show you how to draw a scribble person.* Demonstrate by drawing a stick figure using tiny circles repeated over and over with the pencil never leaving the page.
- *When I give you the Start cue, one partner draws a scribble person in some sort of action—jumping, running, etc.*
- *When I cue again, the second partner takes the pencil and adds a second character that in some way interacts with the first character.*
- *You don't discuss this at all. You each will create your own scribble person.*
- Allow 60 seconds for each partner. Have students put pencils down and allow 60 seconds to talk with partners about what the people might be doing.

Debrief: You might wish to have students share their creations, name the scribble people, or even write about them in a Language Arts task.

Pencil and Paper

Subjects: Art; Language Arts

Partners

Props: One piece of paper and several different writing tools per student

Note:
- It is not necessary to know actual sign language; students are adept at creating understandable hand signals and facial expressions.
- Adding numbers and details to the suggestions make them more difficult.

46. Sign Me A Picture

Objective: To draw an illustration by interpreting nonverbal language.

- *With your partner you have to communicate in ways other than with words. You might use hand gestures, facial expressions, body movements. Be creative.*
- *Decide who is A and who is B.*
- *Partner A will give the nonverbal directions. Partner B, you will try to draw whatever A is trying to get you to draw.*
- *Artist Henri Matisse said, "Creativity takes courage." I want you to show courage in attempting this task. In other words, don't be afraid to just draw.*
- *I will tell all the Partner A's what that image will be.* To keep it simple and to save thinking time, tell each Partner A what the image should be.
- *Every Partner B, please put your head down and close your eyes while I share the image with the your partner.* Show the words quickly then give the Start cue.
- If students are having trouble, help them by suggesting a few ideas, such as finger-in-the-air drawing, tapping parts of the body to show numbers, or nodding/shaking the head for right/wrong responses. Remind them that this is just for fun.
- After about two minutes, give the Stop cue. *Was that difficult? Why or why not?*

Debrief: Discuss how good/bad different pairs were in achieving the desired illustration, and how their work might have been improved. Laugh together at the (mostly) funny representations.

Extended Debrief: Discuss the challenges met by people who cannot hear or speak. There is room for extension of this task into Language Arts, Health, Social Studies, etc. Or carry out an Internet search and learn how to use actual sign language to sign phrases such as "thank you" or "I love you."

* * *

Sample Illustrations

- a flower
- a jacket (with a zipper, with 5 buttons)
- a vehicle
- a house
- a starry night sky
- an apple tree with 7 apples
- a bus with 6 visible windows

Pencil and Paper

Subjects: Health & Wellness; Language Arts; Social Studies

Individual

Props: Lined paper and a writing tool for each student

Note: Studies have shown that grateful thinking improves mood, reduces anxiety, has a calming effect, and is strongly related to well-being—all positive byproducts of this refocuser.

47. The Happy Gratefuls

Objective: To jot down the people/situations/items you are grateful for.

- *We all have things we are grateful for—Happy Gratefuls. Even when you might think you have nothing good going for you, there is someone or something that is a Happy Grateful in your life.*
- *For the next two minutes, quickly jot down any of your Happy Gratefuls that come to mind. You might think of only one thing, situation, person, or pet—it doesn't matter.*
- *When I give the Start cue, put yourself grateful mode and let yourself go.*
- *You have to work quickly, so don't try to pick the best or the perfect Happy Grateful. Just jot down as many as you can in the two minutes.*
- Give the Start cue. If you notice anyone not writing, approach with suggestions; e.g., *Your mom? Your dad? Your friend? Your strong body? Your home with a warm bed?*
- Give the Stop cue and invite students to share one of their Happy Gratefuls.

Debrief: Invite students to share how they feel after this activity.

Extended Debrief: An excellent follow-up activity is to do an Internet search for quotes about gratefulness. Have students choose their 10 favorite quotes and write in more depth about one of them.

3

Up and At 'Em

Because these refocusers are readily visible to all, they are more entertaining than those in the previous chapter. Their magic lies in the beautiful hyperactivity-reduction fostered by the restricted, guided movements.

The 3-Minute Motivators in this chapter get the students moving. Get Active refocusers are done silently at individual desks, and tend to be slightly less active than the Get Involved and Sound and Movement activities. The Get Involved refocusers are also silent, but usually require acting or reacting to others, and tend to make use of bigger, more lively movements. Activities in the Sound and Movement section make positive use of both sounds or words and big actions.

Get Active

The 3-Minute Motivators in this section are designed to provide students with a controlled escape for energy while energizing those who might be bored or sleepy. In most cases, students remain seated at their own desks, and are involved in innovative, teacher-led, movement-based activities—on their own. They will take part in a variety of low-risk activities that will challenge them to be creative and focused. Cognition, imagination, short-term memory, and fine motor skills all come into play, as well as accurate looking, listening to directions, and deciphering nonverbal communication cues.

- Most of these 3-Minute Motivators are individual pursuits; students perform them on their own; however, a few involve working in pairs and in some instances individuals become a component of the whole-class activity (e.g., Thunderstorm, page 56).
- Get Active motivators are largely silent activities, and teachers will need to reinforce this aspect. Communication can be ongoing, but it is nonverbal communication. Before beginning the movement, reinforce that it is a silent activity. Occasionally sounds might be suggested, but all the refocusers in this section can be effectively carried out without them.
- Teachers will probably choose Get Active refocusers if they want to engage students actively, yet minimize student interactions. However, whole-class discussions can easily follow any of the activities.
- In most cases, no props are needed for Get Active refocusers. If props are needed, they are minimal and readily available; i.e., a coin or a piece of paper to write on.

Subject: Any, especially where fine motor control is required

Individual

Note: This is a good hand exercise; using it prior to a lengthy writing exercise could be useful.

48. Open–Shut–Shake

Objective: To mimic increasingly difficult hand movements.

- *Sit straight in your desk, feet on the floor, eyes on me.*
- *I am going to model a hand movement that will be either opening/closing hands (O/C), or a shake of the hands.* Demonstrate by opening/closing hands once and shaking loose hands twice.
- *Your job is to repeat exactly what I have done.*
- Begin simply: e.g., three shakes, three O/C. Then increase difficulty: e.g., one O/C, two shakes, four O/C, one shake, etc. The increasing difficulty keeps students on their toes.
- To bump up the action, invite students to take turns being the leader.

Showcase: Invite students to prepare, in their own time, a demonstration Open–Shut–Shake routine, perhaps done to music.

Subjects: Language Arts; Social Studies

Individual

49. Puppet Master

Objective: To experience being controlled by marionette strings.

- *Sit quietly at your desk, feet on floor, arms draped across desk, head on desk.*
- *Close your eyes.*
- *You are going to become a marionette, a puppet on strings.*
- *I am the puppeteer. When I tell you I am pulling a certain string, you move only that part of your body.*
- *Relax completely. You are a puppet with no bones. Breathe deeply.*
- *I am gently pulling your right arm up…and down*
- *Your left arm up.* Continue in this manner until all body parts have been gently raised or moved. Be sure to raise unusual parts, such as elbows, wrists, left ear, and so on.
- *Now I am going to pull several strings at once and you will sit up—carefully. I haven't lifted your head yet.*
- *Now your head.*
- Continue as long as desired or until students tire.
- *Feel your strange body. It is being held up only by strings.*
- *Now I am very gently wiggling the strings. You stay seated, but your body moves in tiny wiggles—all over.*
- *Now I'm going to cut the strings and you will all gently drop back to your desk—when I tell you. NOW!*

Debrief: *Tell a neighbor what it felt like to be moved by a puppeteer.*

Showcase: An entire group of choreographed marionettes, moving to music, makes an excellent demonstration piece for concerts or parents' nights.

Get Active

Subjects: Science; Social Studies
Individual

Note: Remind students that they are to remain quiet throughout, and to concentrate on their own actions.

50. Glass Blower

Objective: To imagine blowing glass into something beautiful.

- *Sit quietly, feet on floor, hands on desk.*
- *You are going to be a glass blower. Imagine that on your desk there is a lump of soft glass.*
- *Pick it up. Feel it. It's like squishy clay.*
- *Now make your hands into gentle fists like a tube. Bring them to your mouth to blow as if you were blowing through the tube.* Demonstrate by putting the thumb side of one fist against your mouth, and the thumb side of the other behind it to form a hollow tube.
- *Your glass lump is attached to the end of your tube. Blow gently through your hands and the glass will start to take form. Blow gently; if you blow too hard, you will destroy the glass.*
- *Concentrate on what you are making with your glass. Are you making a vase? A glass animal? A beautiful ornament? A crystal ball? Look at it as you blow—slowly, carefully.*
- Keep cueing them like this for 30 to 60 seconds.
- *Now your glass item is complete. Very carefully put your tube down by releasing your hands, and gently remove the object from the end. Be careful. It's warm; it's very delicate.*
- *Set it on your desk and look at it. Isn't it beautiful? Look at all the detail. Memorize what it looks like.*
- *You made this by being calm and gentle.*

Showcase: Students, in turn, quickly tell what they created.

Follow-up: Students write about or illustrate personal glass creations.

Get Active

Subjects: Health & Wellness; Phys Ed
Individual

51. Life Rhythms

Objective: To connect speed of tapping with different life emotions.

- *Sit straight in your desk, feet on the floor, eyes on me.*
- *We are going to tap our desks with fingers (or clap our hands) very slowly, a little faster, or very quickly, depending on the cues I give you.* Model very slow taps, then very quick taps.
- *Some feelings or emotions feel like they slow us down—like fear, for instance. It might tap slowly.* Model and let students copy.
- *But excitement would be very fast.* Model and let students copy.
- *Some feelings might be very soft taps, while others might be hard taps. It's up to you to choose. I might choose soft and slow for a feeling like worry.*
- *Now I will say an emotion and you will tap the speed you think best describes that feeling. This is not a contest—everyone might tap different speeds, and that's okay. Just tap for yourself and keep the speed you choose until I say a different emotion.*

Debrief: It might be a good idea to briefly discuss the correlation between the rhythms the students tapped and the rhythm of their hearts. This could lead to a lesson on how we handle emotions and, therefore, protect our hearts.

52. Thunderstorm

Objective: To create the sounds of a storm using the hands and feet.

- *Sit straight in your desk, feet on the floor, eyes on me.*
- *We are going to create a thunderstorm right here in the class, but we are going to remain calm throughout the storm.*
- *Begin by rubbing your palms together.* Continue for about 10 seconds. *This is the wind.*
- *Now change to finger snapping.* Continue for about 10 seconds. *This is the rain.*
- *Now clap—the rain getting harder. Keep breathing slowly. Stay calm and peaceful, even though it is storming.*
- *Keep clapping and add feet stamping—harder rain and thunder. Harder! HARDER! But stay calm.*
- Continue for no more than 20 seconds, then reverse the sequence.
- *Thunder has stopped!*
- *Rain is lessening. Gentle rain.* Snapping gets slower and lighter.
- *Wind turns to breeze.* Progress from quickly rubbing hands together to slowly rubbing and eventually stopping.
- *Listen to the silence following the storm.* Allow 30 seconds of silent listening.

Debrief: *Did this sound like a thunderstorm to you? Why or why not?* Ask if storms make students excited, scared, anxious, etc. Invite discussion about ways to stay calm in a storm; this can be a literal or figurative discussion depending on the age of your students.

Get Active

Subjects: Health & Wellness; Language Arts

Individual

Props: One balloon and one marker per student

Note: This refocuser has cathartic properties; the popping of a balloon with something written/drawn on it provides a jolt of adrenalin and subsequent stress relief.

53. Blasting Balloons

Objective: To blow up, write on, and break balloons

- *When I give the Start cue, blow up the balloon and tie it.* Do this step before giving more directions, checking that all students have their balloons tied.
- *Now take your markers and write or draw something on your balloons that indicates _____.* Choose words or a simple illustration.
- Allow about 30 seconds for this. It is a quick, spontaneous activity.
- *Now the real fun begins. When I give the cue, break your balloon as quickly as possible, using anything you have that will burst it: scissors, a paper clip, a pencil…whatever.*
- *Before I give that cue, think about what you have written/drawn on the balloon. Realize that, when you break the balloon, you are sending that feeling or idea away. You are making it go away with a bang.* This is an important fact to share with students; they need to be encouraged to make the association between the balloons breaking and the thoughts dissipating. But remind them that, although the negative thought has been burst, it's possible the original negative situation remains.
- Cue to break the balloons

Debrief: Discuss what it felt like to break the balloons that had negative thoughts or feelings on them.

Sample Balloon Words/Drawings

- in-class situation, such as frustration with peers/partners/teacher
- face of someone with whom you are upset/angry/annoyed
- something that frightens/confuses/annoys you
- a rule that is upsetting to you

Get Active

Subject: Any
Individual as part of Whole Class

Notes:
- Since this refocuser involves moving a fair bit, be sure students have sufficient room beside their desks, or use an open area of the room.
- Students love this activity. It is a good opportunity to give small prizes (see page 19) to the last ones standing.

54. Fast Freeze

Objective: To copy actions but freeze on cue.

- *The fun here is that you get to move and then freeze instantly.*
- *I'll be the leader to start. You will all stand and copy everything I do, exactly when and how I do it.*
- *When I give the Stop cue, freeze in whatever position you are in. That position must match exactly the position I am frozen in, or you will be out and have to sit down.*
- *This is an elimination game. Once you are out, you become a judge. You will watch everyone still standing to see if they freeze exactly like the leader as soon as the Stop cue is given.*
- Practice once. Do movements such as arms waving, knees lifting, etc. Freeze at a point where some students may not be in sync with you.
- Now invite students to be leaders. They will initiate moving in imaginative ways, allowing you the freedom to stop them when you see an opportunity.

Get Active

Subject: Any as a source of words
Individual as part of Whole Class

Props: Word lists

Prep: Compile lists of words that will ignite emotion in students.

Note: This rapid-thinking/rapid-reacting activity serves to stimulate and also defuse heightened inappropriate energy.

55. Cold–Hot–Not

Objective: To make instant decisions about whether something is Cold, Hot, or Not (neither), and to make appropriate movements.

- *This is a fast-thinking game.*
- Model the movements: *You will use thumbs-up, to show* Hot; *thumbs-down to show* Cold; *and no-thumbs (just fists) to show* Not, *which could mean "either," "neither," or "both." Whatever you use, hold it high in the air.*
- With the class, practice the three movements once. *If I call out something, like "ice," that is cold, show thumbs-down. If I call something like "fire," show thumbs-up. If I call something like "coffee" that can be hot or cold, you use no-thumbs, just fists.*
- *You have to pay close attention and think quickly.*
- Remind students that not all will respond in the same way, and that's okay. For example, for the word "opera," the teacher might respond *Hot* if she likes opera, while students might respond *Cold* if they dislike it.
- With younger children, use concrete words. With older children, increase the difficulty by using more abstract words; explain that their responses depend on how they feel about the item or situation.

* * *

Sample Concrete Words

- Winter, fall, spring, summer, sun, moon
- Niagara Falls, Pacific Ocean, Arctic Sea
- Sauna, shower, swimming pool, bathtub
- Foods; e.g., ice cream, spaghetti, soup, hot chocolate
- Campfire, candle flame, oven, freezer
- Steam, smoke, tornado, hurricane

Sample Abstract Words

- Homework, housework, chores
- Any school subject
- Friends, enemies, family, relatives, teachers, coaches
- Kinds of music; e.g., rap, hip-hop, classical, country, rock, pop
- Current TV shows or movies
- Current TV or movie stars, athletes, famous people
- Clothing fads or name brands; e.g., Adidas, Nike
- Popular fast food; e.g., hamburgers, tacos, milkshakes
- Familiar activities; e.g., going to the movies, going skating, talking on the phone
- Popular technology; e.g., MP3 player, smart phone, tablet
- Hairstyles; e.g., ponytail, buzz cut, brightly colored hair, Mohawk, dreadlocks, shaved head

Get Active

Subjects: Art; Science
Individual

56. Stuck!

Objective: To experience being "stuck" to the desk.

- *Sit comfortably in your desk, feet on the floor.*
- *Stretch your arms across the desk and put your head down on the desk. Get as comfortable as possible, with as much of your body touching the desktop as possible.*
- *Listen carefully. When I give you the Start cue, you are suddenly going to be completely stuck to your desk. Your feet will be stuck to the floor.*
- *You will need to listen for my cues before you'll be able to get unstuck.*
- *Cue. You are totally stuck. You can't lift anything. Try to lift your head. Impossible! Try each arm—stuck fast!*
- *For the next few seconds you will try unsuccessfully to lift different parts of your body, but you are too tightly stuck.* Wait for about 15 seconds. If any student succeeds in "lifting" a body part, just remind them all that they are too stuck to move.
- *Feel the heaviness of your head stuck to the desk. Feel the weight of your arms…hands…legs. You might be able to move your knees, but your feet don't move at all.*
- Continue in this manner for up to two minutes.
- *The glue is starting to weaken. You can lift one hand…one arm…*
- Continue giving "unstuck" cues until students are sitting upright again.

- *One final thing is stuck—your backside. You are stuck to your seat and will stay that way until the end of the lesson on _____. Return to the lesson being taught before the refocuser.*

Debrief: Ask how many students actually had a sense of being stuck. You might wish to discuss possible reasons for this. Depending on the age of students, this can lead to a discussion about being "stuck" figuratively, in specific situations, life patterns, etc.

Get Active

Subject: Any as a source of statements

Individual

Props: True/False sentences from any subject area.

Prep: You can make up the statements on the spot or select from a bank of statements you have previously prepared.

Notes:
- This refocuser readily adapts to subject review.
- Another way to use False Freeze is with rhyming (*move*) and non-rhyming (*freeze*) words.

57. False Freeze

Objective: To stand up or sit down according to whether or not what the teacher says is true; to "freeze" if a statement is false.

- *Sit sideways in your chair so that you can stand up easily and quickly without bumping anyone else.*
- *You have a choice of doing one of three things. You are going to stand up, sit down, or freeze every time I say something*
- *If I say something that is true, like "I am your teacher," and you are sitting as you are now, you must stand up quickly. True statements require you to move, to change position.*
- *If next I say something false, like "I am a car," you must freeze. In other words, stay standing, don't move at all. False statements require you to freeze.*
- *Then, if I say, "You are students"—that's true—you move again, and sit back down since you are already standing up.*
- *So you* move *every time I say something true. If I say something not true, you* freeze *where you are.*
- *If you get caught off guard, not sure if a statement is true or false, you might have to freeze halfway up or halfway down.*
- Provide sentences slowly at first; gradually increase speed so that students are really moving. This sounds easier than it is. Kids love it, and teachers can review basic subject concepts readily.

Extended Debrief: Statements with "debatable" or "sometimes" responses can lead to effective discussions and writing tasks.

*   *   *

Sample T/F Statements

- Boys are usually taller than girls.
- Ice melts when heated.
- The sky can be orange.
- Birds fly.
- Dogs meow.
- Chocolate is always brown.
- Blueberries are purple.
- Applesauce is made from pears.
- Erasers remove ink.
- Cows drink milk.
- Coffee is always hot.
- A pencil is made of wood.
- Teachers are always female.
- The gym is used for assemblies.
- Ink is blue.
- Cell phones hurt your eyes.
- Video games are always good for you.

58. Balancing Act

Objective: To balance in various positions.

- *For this game you will need to stand quietly beside your desk.*
- *I will ask you to balance in some different ways. Listen carefully and hold the balance once you get it.*
- *A good tip is to look at a spot on the floor about one body-length in front of you. Focus on that imaginary spot, and it will be easier to keep your balance.*
- *You will be competing with yourself; try to increase the time you can hold a position each time we do it.*
- *If you lose your balance, take a breath and re-balance.*
- Have students hold each balance, beginning with 15 seconds and working up to 60 seconds.
- Challenge students to come up with other balance poses.

*   *   *

Use your judgement as to the difficulty of the balances you have them attempt. The following balances are listed in order of difficulty, from easiest to most challenging:

1. Simple Stork: one foot on other knee; arms out to sides
2. Complex Stork: one foot on other knee; hands clasped above head
3. Simple Skater: one leg extended behind; arms to sides
4. Harder Skater: one leg extended behind; arms pushed out in front, hands clasped
5. Complex Skater: one leg extended behind; arms tightly presses to sides
6. Simple Pretzel: one leg behind, foot held with opposite hand (i.e., right hand holds left foot); other arm out straight
7. Complex Pretzel: same as Simple Pretzel, but with other arm behind back
8. Easy Squat: squat down with one leg extended in front, arms wide
9. Complex Squat: same as Easy Squat but with arms behind back

59. Bump on the Head

Objective: To be a nail or a screw and experience being pounded or screwed into a piece of wood.

- *Stand quietly beside your desk.*
- *When I give the Start cue, you will become a huge nail (screw).*
- *Every time I cue you (clap my hands, etc.), a huge hammer (screwdriver) will hit you on the head (turn you) and push you a little farther into the ground.*
- *Remember that your feet will be the first to disappear, then a little more with each bang.*
- *You'll end up squatting as close to the floor as possible. It will take about ten hits (turns) for this.*

Get Active
Subjects: Language Arts; Music
Individual as part of Whole Class

Note: Although this refocuser involves students watching each other, it remains an individual pursuit.

60. Knocking Knees

Objective: To maintain a continually expanding sequence of clap/knee actions.

- *For this game you must turn sideways in your chairs.*
- *We are going to keep a rhythm using just our hands and knees.*
- *I'll start you off. Then I'll call a name, and that person will add another movement to the sequence—just do it, don't say what you are doing. We'll keep building until we can't remember anymore.*
- *If I call your name and you can't think of anything, just say, "Pass."*
- *Let's start with this:* Clap hands once, hit knees twice.

Repeat this sequence a few times before calling on a student.

* * *

Sample Movements

- Bump knees together two or three times
- Click fingers and lift knees alternately
- Open and shut knees several times
- Clap hands on or under knees
- Stamp feet: stamp in/out/in/out, front/back, etc.
- Hit opposite knees; i.e., right hand to left knee, left hand to right knee
- Clap to the side, above, behind back, far out in front

61. Wide–Hide

Objective: To move rapidly from a standing, wide stance to a curled-up, hiding position.

- *First we will stand beside our desks and try to take up as much room as possible without moving. Spread your arms; stand wide like you are hugging a huge ball.*
- *Now, quickly go from that Wide position—an embracing or welcoming position—to becoming as small as you can, all curled up as if trying to disappear in your desk. This is your Hide position.*
- *Now sit normally.*
- *I will say something. If it's something you like or feel good about, immediately get Wide and embrace it. If it's something you dislike, feel badly about, or are afraid of, quickly get into the Hide position and try to be invisible. There can be no in-between. You have to choose either Wide or Hide.*
- *Remember that everyone will have different reactions. There is no right or wrong answer to any of the suggestions. You may want to hide from all of them, or you may want to get huge and embrace all of them.*

*   *   *

Sample Words

- Freezing weather
- Warm sandy beach
- Amusement park
- Pollution
- Foul-smelling garbage dump
- Rocket to space
- Boys/Girls
- Homework

- Ice-cream sundaes
- Brussel sprouts
- Pizza
- Dancing
- Mountain climbing
- Deep-sea diving
- Going to the dentist
- Monster (horror) movies

Get Active

Subject: Math (probability)

Individual

Props: A coin; pencil and paper

62. Heads or Tails

Objective: To select Heads or Tails ten times and check your luck.

- *On your paper, write the numbers 1 to 10 in a vertical column.*
- *Now choose Heads or Tail ten times; write* H *or* T *beside each number.*
- *I will toss the coin and you will check your guesses.*
- *If you have* Heads *written beside the number, stand up* before *I toss. In this way we'll all know who guessed right for each number.*
- *Stand if you have* Heads *beside number one. Toss the coin; tell students who obviously have the correct guess to give themselves a checkmark beside that number.*
- *Continue for all ten tosses, then check for winners; i.e., whoever guessed correctly the most times. If too many are winners the first time through, play off the winners against each other and invite non-players to take turns tossing the coin.*

Debrief: Discuss probability and why it's impossible to predict when heads or tails will fall.

Extended Debrief: Discuss the difficulties involved in gambling as related to this topic.

63. Ice Cube

Objective: To experience (in your mind) the feeling of having an ice cube dropped down your back.

- *Sit tall in your desk, feet on the floor, eyes on me.*
- *Something is going to happen to you—but in your imagination, in your mind. It might be something that has already happened to some of you.*
- *When I give the Start cue, a big, cold ice cube will be dropped down your back. You won't be able to sit still—you'll have to wiggle or do whatever you can to get it out.*
- *You won't be able to get it out until I give the Stop cue. At that time, the ice cube will be completely melted.*
- *You might need to stand up, but you can't leave your desk area.*
- Cue to start; continue side coaching for up to a minute.

Debrief: *Could you* really *feel the ice melting in your shirt? What did it feel like?*

Showcase: If any students were particularly interesting or amusing, invite them to share.

Get Active

Subjects: Health & Wellness; Phys Ed; Science
Individual

Note: This is a cardio activity that temporarily increases heart rate and serves to reduce stress.

64. Fast Feet

Objective: To provide an escape for excess energy by quickly, silently "running" feet.

- *Stand beside your desk. Remember to stay in your own space bubble.*
- *When I give the Start cue, quickly and quietly run on the spot. Move your feet as fast as possible for a few seconds. Then, on cue, stop the fast feet and change to slow, silent marching on the spot.*
- Alternate fast/slow every 10 seconds.
- *During the fast-feet portion, bend over slightly.*
- *During the slow-march portion, stand as tall as possible.*
- Continue alternating fast feet/slow march—10 seconds each, for up to two minutes. Model moving feet fast without noise or forward movement.

65. In Your Arms

Objective: To change focus by concentrating on an imaginary object.

- *Sit tall and get ready to have some fun.*
- *I am going to put imaginary items in your arms. Without getting up, you will have to hold them until I tell you to put them down.*
- *Every time I give the Stop cue, the item will change.*
- *You have to do this without making a sound. If whatever you are holding is painful, you'll have to make a silent scream. If it is tickling you, you'll have to laugh silently.*
- Provide the cue and keep changing the items. You can return to a previous item at any time, to keep the students on their toes.

Debrief: Discuss times when students might have had to hold on to something that was difficult to clutch.

*   *   *

Sample Items

- a squirming baby
- a large burning coal
- a big block of ice
- a mound of green jelly
- a massive balloon, too big to get your arms around
- a big, beautiful, fragile bubble
- a valuable vase that is heavy and very tall
- four tiny, wiggly puppies
- a very long, very big snake
- a bunch of beautiful but prickly roses
- a handful of very sharp knives

Get Active

Subjects: Math; Phys Ed; Science

Individual

Note: Moving different body parts in circles is a valuable fitness trick to loosen joints and relieve tightness due to stress, fatigue, or frustration.

66. Circles, Circles, Circles

Objective: To move different body parts in circles.

- *Sit comfortably at your desk.*
- *When I cue you, draw imaginary circles with the part of your body I call.*
- *Try to draw a complete circle with each part. Pay attention to what that feels like.*
- *The circle can be big or little—it's up to you.*
- Start with easy parts, such as wrists or shoulders. Then proceed through the entire body if time permits.

*   *   *

Suggestion for Body Parts to Circle

- Shoulders: forward and backward
- Head: carefully and slowly
- Nose, ears
- Chest
- Backside: stand for this
- Toes, knees, legs, feet
- Tongues, eyes
- Fingers: one at a time
- Trunk: move through the waist
- Entire body: stand, feet grounded

Get Active

Subject: Science

Individual

67. Melt

Objective: To melt into nothing, as a candle or snowman would.

- *Stand beside your desk.*
- *Stand as tall as possible. You are a snowman (candle).*
- *When I give the Start cue, you will start to melt. Remember to melt from the top down—very, very slowly.*
- *See if you can take a full 60 seconds to melt into a puddle on the floor, or draped over your desk. I will tell you as the time passes.*
- Cue to start.
- Tell students when each 10 seconds have passed.
- Once they are on the floor, say, *Now you are just a puddle of water (of wax). Relax. Don't move. When I give the cue you will slowly return to sitting in your desk.*

Debrief: Discuss what it felt like to melt.

Showcase: If any students were particularly interesting or creative in their endeavor, invite them to share.

Get Involved

The 3-Minute Motivators in this section call for moderate to active physical involvement on the part of students. The refocusers require them to stand beside or behind their desks and move in some fanciful manner, usually with partners or in small groups; i.e., involved with others). In some cases they will actually move around the room. However, these are silent refocusers, as no talk is allowed; this helps to control any heightened energy that might accompany the activities.

The nature of these motivators makes them excellent for very active children who need to burn off a bit of energy before more focused seatwork or a listening activity. Older students (up to and including high school) still benefit from getting up and moving when they start to feel or act bored or sleepy.

Because students are acting or doing, they are, in fact, representing, one of the key components of the Language Arts curriculum. They are also listening closely to cues from the teacher. Short-term memory and imagination as well as cognition, come into play as students engage in the various activities. If showcasing is involved, instant visualization is added to the repertoire of areas being addressed.

- Most students enjoy these fairly active exploits. However, if a student is shy, challenged in any way, or just feeling "out of it," it's a good idea to promote the use of the Pass—the right to "sit this one out as long as you refocus with everyone else when it's over."
- Remember to reinforce the silent nature of these activities; often the fun is greater simply because no oral communication is allowed.

Get Involved

Subject: Math

Partners

Note: This is a favorite refocuser that students never seem to tire of. Just remind them that no oral communication is allowed.

68. Number Shakes

Objective: To achieve a specific number by shaking fists and extending fingers.

- *Turn to face your partner (your neighbor, the person behind you, etc.).*
- *Sit comfortably with your feet on the floor.*
- *This is like the game Rock, Paper, Scissors. You shake your fists three times and, on the fourth time, you both open your hands at the same time. But instead of making the sign for rock, paper, or scissors, you will hold out as many fingers as you want.*
- *I will call a number and your goal is to try to shake the number I call. For example, if I call 3, then one partner would need one finger and the other would need two. Or one partner might shake no fingers (that is, keep his/her fist closed), while the partner puts out three fingers.*
- *Keep track of how many tries you and your partner need to reach the magic number. As soon as you get the number, raise your hands.*
- This gets a bit competitive, as pairs all want to be the first to get the number. You can play up this competition or not, depending on your students. It's usually a good idea to stop when several pairs get the number, then start again with a new number. Bigger numbers can involve using all four hands.
- To increase the difficulty level for older students, try positive and negative integers. One partner is positive, the other negative; together they must come up with the called number. Or use with subtraction (subtract one number from another to get the called number), multiplication, or division. Lots of variables are possible.
- Another alternative is to challenge two or more students to shake exactly the same number. In other words, how many tries does it take for both to shake, for example, threes?

Get Involved

Subject: Any as source of words

Partners

Props: Paper and writing tools

Prep: Compile a list of words complex enough to be challenging and not immediately discernible.

Notes:

- This is a good vocabulary review activity. If students are having trouble unscrambling, give a subject clue; e.g., *It comes from Social Studies*.
- Most teachers have used this technique, but tossing it into a lesson in the form of a 3-Minute Motivator gives it whole new life and appeal. The competitive nature encourages and stimulates students.

69. All Shook Up

Objective: To unscramble letters to form familiar vocabulary words.

- *In this game, you and your partner figure out a word from the letters that have been "all shook up" and put on the board/overhead/chart/interactive whiteboard.*
- *This is a word game. You are competing with the other pairs to see who can unscramble it first. You can talk quietly with your partner to work out the word together.*
- *Start when I give the cue. As soon as you have the word, raise your hands and put your pencils down. I'll watch to see who the winners are.*
- Cue to start and watch closely. Stop the activity when a few partners have the word. Repeat with another word if time allows.

Props: One small balloon per student.

Note: It might be because of the anticipated loud noise or the adrenalin rush that accompanies it, but bursting balloons is fun. It reduces tension and frustration very quickly.

70. Balloon Battles

Objective: To quickly blow up a balloon, play fight, and then burst it.

- Pass out a balloon to each student. Caution students not to blow them up yet.
- *When I cue you to start, you will have 30 seconds to blow up your balloons and tie them off. Go!* Wait about 30 seconds.
- *Now turn to a neighbor and play fight by holding your balloons by the ties and hitting them against each other. Don't break the balloons, just bat them together carefully. Go!* Allow only 20–30 seconds for this; it can become too aggressive if too much time is given.
- Cue to stop.
- *Now you have 30 seconds to burst your balloons, in any way you can. Use whatever you have available at your desks. Go!*

Get Involved

Subject: Math
Partners

Props: One piece of paper and a writing tool per student.

71. Lucky Hi/Lo

Objective: To test your luck by trying to match the high or low called by the teacher.

- This is like Number Shakes (page 66) in that it follows the Rock, Paper, Scissors process of shaking closed fists three times and opening on the fourth shake.
- *Begin by writing your name and your partner's name side by side on a piece of paper to keep score. Use a little part of your notebook if you like.* You can supply scrap paper, as long as the distribution doesn't take long.
- *Sit facing your partner, feet on the floor.*
- *Make fists, and shake three times. On the fourth shake you will open your fists to hold out any number of fingers out you choose.* Allow a couple of practices.
- *Now comes the game part. After you open your fists, I will be calling "High" or "Low." The person whose fingers match what I call gets a point under his or her name.* Model, using both your hands. Hold up one finger on one hand and three on the other and demonstrate which hand is high and which is low.
- *If you both show the same number, neither of you gets the point.*
- *To make it fair, I won't watch you as you open your fists.* Turn away.
- Do the "One, two, three" count with them, then say either "High" or "Low." Make the calling random. Avoid just alternating, as students will be quick to pick up on this.

Debrief: You can reinforce the idea of probability (or improbability) in any game involving luck.

Get Involved

Subjects: Any that use sequencing skills; e.g., Language Arts (events in a story), Math (counting) Science (steps in an experiment)

Partners

72. Monkey See, Monkey Do

Objective: To create a sequence of interesting arm and hand movements.

- *Turn to face your partner.*
- *Sit straight in your chairs, feet on floor, arms resting on desktops.*
- *Decide who's A and who's B.*
- *Partner A will do an arm or hand movement, something simple like this.* Model opening and closing hands twice quickly, then rolling one shoulder.
- *Partner B will copy the movement, then add another movement, like this.* Model opening/closing hands twice, rolling the shoulder, then quietly clapping three times.
- *You will keep taking turns adding movements until I give you the Stop cue.*
- *Try to remember all the actions in sequence. After the Stop cue, you and your partner will go through the whole sequence together.*
- *This is a silent activity; no talking, just doing.*

Debrief: Discuss the importance of correct sequencing in the subject being studied.

Showcase: This is an activity students love to share. Allow a few pairs (as many as time allows) to demonstrate their complete sequence in unison.

       *   *   *

Sample Movements

- Snap fingers
- Use imaginary lassos
- Tap knuckles together
- Tap desks, knees, forehead, ears
- Shake index fingers
- Make punching moves
- Roll shoulders, shrug
- Circle elbows backward, like wings
- Wiggle fingers

Get Involved

Subject: Any
Individual

Notes:
- This 3-Minute Motivator might seem too childish for any but the youngest students, but I have found all ages (even adults) love the silliness of this activity and the movement and brain relaxation it allows.
- Students will need to be reminded not to infringe on the personal space of others.

73. Body by Color

Objective: To touch specific body parts to specific colors in the room.

- *We are going to move around a bit, so remember each other's personal spaces.*
- *I am going to call out a body part and a color; for example, "Nose, red."*
- *Your job will be to locate something red in the room, then quickly and quietly go to it and put your nose against it.*
- *If it is a small item and someone else is already there, you might have to find a different item.*
- *You can share items if they are big enough, but no talking; just walking and touching body parts to items.*

Notes:

- This is not necessarily a silent activity, as it involves students making musical tones. However, these sounds can be omitted entirely and the activity will still be effective.
- Any refocuser that involves a physical burst of energy like this will work well as a tension/stress reducer.

74. Musical Punching Bags

Objective: To punch imaginary punching bags and attach tones to the punches.

- *Turn to your partner.*
- *Sit with your feet on the floor, facing each other. Make fists.*
- *Imagine a small punching bag hanging right in front of you, but not close to your partner.*
- *Take a few practice punches in the air. Remember to stay out of your partner's punching area.*
- *You and your partner are going to take turns punching a bag that hangs between you. It's a small punching bag but, each time you punch it, the bag makes a musical sound of some sort. Remember it's a small bag, so it's a small sound. You must make the musical tone without opening your lips.* You can model a couple of musical punches.
- *Take turns with the bag. Try to be creative.* Cue to start.
- After 30 to 40 seconds say, *Now take turns copying what your partner did, then adding to that, until you have an interesting combination of punches and sounds.*
- *Pay attention to the most interesting punch–sound combinations you and your partner can come up with. You might be able to share these later.*

Showcase: Invite some pairs to demonstrate punch–sound combinations.

75. Shake It!

Objective: To alternate between moving silently and shaking the entire body vigorously on cue.

- *This game is fun because you get to shake your entire body—just like a dog might shake when it's wet.*
- *But you can only shake everything when I say "Shake it!" The rest of the time, you will shake only the body part I call out.*
- *When I give the Start cue, please stand and walk carefully around the room, being careful of everyone else's personal space.*
- Cue to begin. Alternate body parts with "Shake it!"

* * *

Body Parts to Call

- fingers
- hands
- shoulders
- one foot/leg/arm/knee/elbow
- head
- nose
- hair
- backside

Get Involved

Subject: Science

Partners

Props: Slow music without words; e.g., meditation or yoga music

Note: This activity can also be done without music, but it seems to flow more naturally with it.

76. Magic Mirrors

Objective: To mirror the slow, smooth actions of a peer.

- *Turn to face your partner (your neighbor, the person in front of you) and sit up straight with your feet on the floor.*
- *Your job will be to mirror each other's actions. Whatever your partner does with his or her hands and arms, you do exactly the same.*
- *Remember that a mirror shows the opposite, so if your partner is leading and he or she pulls back, you pull back too, instead of following forward.* Model with a student.
- *Try to be creative. Make big but very slow movements.*
- *You must maintain eye contact! That's the trick here. Don't look at your partner's hands; look only at the eyes. So move* slowly!
- *If you are the leading partner, you are not trying to trick your partner. You are trying to lead and be followed exactly.*
- *Decide who will be the first leader. Start when the music begins. When I give the signal, change leaders.*
- Give the Start cue.
- Allow about 30 seconds, then give the signal to change leaders.

Showcase: This activity lends itself to quickly sharing a sequence of movements with the class; encourage sharing if, and only if, a pair wishes to do so.

Get Involved

Subject: Language Arts

Partners

Props: Paper and writing tools for all students

77. Tap It to Me

Objective: To figure out words by spelling them into a partner's palm.

- *This is a challenge game. You and your partner will challenge the other pairs.*
- *I will give you a word, but only one person in each pair will see it.*
- *That partner will spell it into the palm of the other partner by tapping the correct number of times.*

  > *For example, if the word was* cat, *I'd first tap three times, because C is the third letter of the alphabet. My partner would write down the letter C.*
  > *As soon as my partner writes the letter C, I go on the next letter. I tap once for A. My partner writes A.*

- *If my partner guesses the word based on just two letters, he or she can write the whole word. If it's correct, I can go on to the next word, and continue until we have all the words.*
- *If my partner makes a mistake, I shake my head. Remember—no talking! And no drawing of the letters in your palms.*
- *I will put the words on the board.* (Choose two to five words) *One partner has to turn now so as not to see the board.*
- Difficulty can be determined by your choice of words. It can also be increased by writing a complete short sentence rather than single words.
- *If your partner loses track or you tap the wrong number, moving your hands side-to-side lets the other person know to start again.* Demonstrate.
- Cue to start. Stop when the first pair indicates completion of all words.

Props: Blindfolds

Notes:

- If you have a class set of blindfolds (see page 48) you can use them. If not, trust students to keep their eyes closed by explaining that this is the only way they can truly experience this refocuser.
- This refocuser can be taken out of the actual classroom if desired; e.g., "Lead to the washroom, the office, the…"

78. Blind Walk

Objective: To lead or be led around the room.

- *Decide which partner is* B *(Blind) and which is* L *(Leader). You will change halfway through.*
- *Partner B, you are blind. Put on the blindfold or close your eyes. No peeking.*
- *When I cue you to start, Partner L, carefully lead your partner wherever I tell you to go.*
- *Partner B, you must trust your partner. Partner L, you must be very trustworthy. You cannot talk. You must lead by giving gentle physical cues, such as touching your partner's right shoulder to turn right, gently pulling your partner's hand to go forward, standing right in front of your blind partner if he or she is about to walk into something.*
- *Remember, Partner L, you are in control. Also keep in mind that in a few minutes you will be the blind partner.*
- Provide the locations to go to (see below). All pairs will be heading to the same place, so it must be big enough to accommodate all the students; e.g., "the front of the room," as opposed to "John's desk."
- Have students switch positions after about 60 seconds

Debrief: Discuss what it was like to be totally dependent on another; to be totally responsible for another. Relate these two situations to real life.

* * *

Sample Locations/Directions

- five steps straight ahead/back/to the left/right
- to the back/front/side of the room
- out the door and back in
- ten steps away from your desk and then back
- to the washrooms/office/library/

Note:

- This activity is a favorite with young children, and they are extremely creative when it comes to acting the opposites.
- Point out to students that either response is acceptable for any of the cues. Our responses are determined by many factors; what makes you a teddy bear one time can just as easily make you a grizzly bear the next. With older students this makes for an excellent discussion.

79. Teddy or Grizzly

Objective: To react to teacher-provided cues as either a teddy bear or a grizzly bear, and to try to remember partner's reactions.

- *All of us are attracted to or like different things; we also have things we are not attracted to, are maybe even afraid of.*
- *For this game, we will call these two different reactions to certain situations teddy bears or grizzly bears. For example, I cry in sad movies. I am a teddy bear in sad movies.* Act like a cute, cuddly teddy bear. *But I get annoyed with bad drivers. I am a grizzly bear when I see bad driving.* Act like a ferocious grizzly bear.
- *When I provide a situation, each of you will reach either as a teddy bear or grizzly bear, depending on how you feel about that particular issue.*
- *You can do whatever you want: claw at the air for the grizzly bear; smile and look cuddly for the teddy bear.*

- *Make sounds you feel fit the two different creatures. Maybe teddy bears coo, hum, or chuckle. Maybe grizzly bears roar, growl, or make some other nasty sound. You decide.*
- *After three or four situations, I will stop cuing. Then your job is to try to remember how your partner reacted to each cue.*
- *To help you remember the cues I will show you them on the board (interactive whiteboard, overhead).*

* * *

Sample Situations

- When I see a hurt animal
- When I visit the dentist/doctor/ hospital
- When someone is being a bully
- When I lose my keys/lunch/ best friend
- When it rains at recess
- When I miss my mom/dad/ brother/friend/pet
- When I stub my toe
- When I get hurt
- When I am sick
- When someone I love is hurt/sick/ afraid
- When we lose a game of soccer/ baseball/hockey

Get Involved

Subjects: Art; Phys Ed; Science
Partners

80. Morphing Madness

Objective: To work with a partner to quietly create, using bodies only, whatever object or being the teacher calls.

- *You and your partner will need to stand together beside your desks, so make sure you have room to move.*
- *This game requires the two of you to use your bodies to make or represent a single thing or being. For example, if I call out "Telephone pole," one of you might stand tall while the other stands facing with arms straight out. Or you might stand back to back, both of you with arms out to the side.*
- *Try it.*
- After each body morph, invite students to stay in form but to look around at peers.

Showcase: Invite any pairs who were particularly creative to share a specific morph with the class.

* * *

Sample Morphs

- Bridge, tower, house, door, gate, fence, church
- Elephant, giraffe, frog, turtle, alligator, bird, butterfly
- Beachball, swing, kite, scissors, footstool, ladder, tub, box
- Rock, tree, waterfall

Notes:

- This game is based on the children's game Simon Says, but I have found it is popular with all ages, even university students.
- This game's power is enhanced with little prizes; see page 19. The prizes are only as good as your enthusiasm for them. Say excitedly, "You win a…" and present the prizes, instead of just handing out the tokens.

81. Do This! Do That!

Objective: To copy only the actions accompanied by the call "Do this!": this is an elimination game.

- *Everyone stand up, please.*
- *I will do an action. If I say, "Do this!" you copy the action.*
- *If I do an action and say "Do that!" you* don't *copy me. In fact, if you move even a tiny bit, you will be out and have to sit down.*
- *The last few standing will be the winners.*
- *If you are out early, your job is to carefully watch the standing people for any hints of movement on the "Do that!"s.*
- Have a practice run. It might be a good idea to stand on a chair so that students can easily see you as you lead.
- There will probably be time to play more than once in the three-minute time. To change it up, invite students to lead.

Note: 3-Minute Motivator As the Circle Turns leads nicely into Lean on Me (page 74). Together they can form an effective anticipatory set for many Health & Wellness topics; e.g., family, peers, friendships, even personality traits, such as trust and integrity.

82. As the Circle Turns

Objective: To move left, right, in, or out while being part of a circle.

- Depending on available space, begin by getting students into either one large group holding hands or several smaller groups (no less than four or five students per group) in a part of the room where they can move the circle in both directions.
- *This is a game that will involve cooperation but no talking.*
- *I will give you movement cues to follow as a group. For example, I might say, "Two steps to the right," and you'd have to do that as a group.*
- *At first I will give the cues slowly, but they will get faster and faster, so you'll need to listen carefully and work together.*
- *No pushing—just cooperating.*
- The idea is to keep the group moving as quickly as possible without endangering anyone. Use your judgement as you see how students behave.

Debrief: Discuss situations in real life where we have to work together and depend on those around us for some sort of support.

*   *   *

Sample Movement Cues

- Any number of lateral steps to either side
- Any number of steps in or out
- Arm movements, such as "Arms up," "Arms in," "Arms down"
- Foot movements, such as "Left foot off the floor," "Right leg shake in the air"
- Level cues, such as "squat as low as possible," "stand on tiptoes"
- Group movements, such as the wave, swaying like a copse of trees in a big wind, turning to the sun like sunflowers

Notes:
- Unlike other Get Involved refocusers, this 3-Minute Motivator involves whispering between partners.
- This refocuser follows nicely on As the Circle Turns (page 73). Together they can form an effective anticipatory set for many Health & Wellness topics; e.g., family, peers, friendships, even personality traits, such as trust and integrity.

83. Lean on Me

Objective: To provide and receive physical support for and from peers.

- *This is a game of trust and cooperation.*
- *I will provide cues from which you will have to figure out a position with your partner.*
- *One partner must always be leaning or using the other for support. For example, if I say, "Back to back," you will stand back to back, but one partner must lean back against the other for support.*
- *You can whisper quietly about it as you find the positions, then hold the position until I give another cue.*
- *You must take turns being the one who is supported.*

Debrief: Quickly discuss what it felt like to be supported by another.

Extended Debrief: Students write or talk metaphorically about being supported.

Showcase: Invite pairs to share a few of the more original poses.

* * *

Sample Position Cues

- Side to side
- Back to side
- Hand to shoulder
- Hand to hand
- Head to head
- One leg off the floor (for one partner; for both partners)
- Foot to hand
- Knee to knee
- Hand to head

Note: Some students do not like being touched. It is important to recognize this and allow them the Pass. You might invite them to be judges/art critics of the final statues.

84. Lump of Clay

Objective: To take turns molding partners into forms.

- *Stand beside your desk with your partner. Decide who's A and who's B.*
- *When I give the Start cue, Partner B will become a very soft lump of clay, and Partner A will become the artist who is going to mold that clay.*
- *Partner B, you must allow A to move your body any way he or she wants to; Partner A, you must protect your clay from hurt or harm, so be careful.*
- *Remember that clay can't talk, so this will be done in silence.*
- *I will know you have created your final piece when A sits down to admire the beautiful artwork.*
- *I will allow you only about two minutes to create your work.*
- *Give Start cue.*
- *After about two minutes, give Stop cue.*
- *If time permits, allow students to change roles and repeat the experience.*

Showcase: Invite students to look around at what others have sculpted.

* * *

Sample Subjects

- a piece of furniture
- a container of some sort
- a plant or tree
- a telephone pole
- a robot or soldier
- a bird or animal
- a church
- a dancer/acrobat/clown

Get Involved

Subjects: Math; Science; Social Studies (ways to meet and greet)

Whole Class

Props: Numbered paper slips, as many as there are students

Prep: Prepare small slips of paper with a number from 1 to 5 on each.

Notes:
- This is an excellent group-formation activity, as it readily creates random groups in an engaging manner.
- Another way to play this game: ask students to secretly choose a number between 1 and 5, and to find others who have chosen the same number.

85. Shake My Hand

Objective: To locate other members of the class who have the same number as you.

- *We are going to use this game to form groups.*
- *This game will involve shaking hands with each other, but in a rather unusual way.*
- *Each of you has a secret number. Don't show anyone your number. Remember it, then discard the paper slip.*
- Distribute numbered slips as evenly as possible. If the number of students is divisible by five, then an equal number of students will have each number. Otherwise, inform students that some groups will have fewer members. Since this is a competitive activity, not knowing in advance how many members a group has make it an unfair challenge.
- *When I give the Start cue, you will walk around the room shaking hands with everyone you meet.*
- *Here's the catch. If your slip had a 3 on it, you must pump everyone's hands three times.* Model pumping your hand/arm three times. *If you had a 1, pump hands only once.*
- *What will happen when a 1 and a 3 meet?* Model with a student so all can see the resistance offered by the 1 when the 3 tries to continue pumping.
- *When you have found someone with the same number as you, connect arms and continue to find the other members of your group.*
- *When your group has all its members, quickly sit down on the floor. First group sitting is the winner.*

Debrief: Ask students what it felt like when they found someone else with the same number.

Extended Debrief: Lengthy discussion about finding someone "just like you" or "not at all like you," or about whatever curriculum connection you have chosen.

Get Involved

Subjects: Math; Phys Ed; Science
Partners

Props: Small beanbags (or rice balloons; see page 138)

Notes:
- Beanbag tossing reinforces self-control, coordination, directionality, focus, coordination, and cooperation.
- This can be done to music, with students tossing and catching in rhythm. Or you can clap a rhythm that keeps changing speed.

86. Beanbag Blitz

Objective: To toss and catch a beanbag.

- *Face your partner. If sitting at your desks makes you too close, one partner can move away, or you can both sit on the floor.*
- *When I give the Start cue, toss your beanbag back and forth, trying to never let it hit the floor or desks. Help your partner by tossing carefully.*
- *Every time I cue, you have to change the way you toss the bag. For example, if I say, "Left hands only," you will have to toss with your left hands.*
- Give the Start cue. Change the method every few seconds.

* * *

Sample Methods

- Both hands
- Either hand
- One partner's right hand, the other's left
- Alternating hands
- Catch with right; toss with left
- Catch with left; toss with right
- Overhand only
- Underhand only
- Tosser eyes closed; catcher eyes open
- Tosser eyes open; catcher eyes closed
- Catch to the side
- Catch in front
- Catch over the head
- Catch with the catcher's back to the tosser
- Clap before catching

Get Involved

Subjects: Phys Ed; Science
Partners

Note: If students are reluctant to participate because of physical closeness, this refocuser can be done individually.

87. Glued to the Ground

Objective: To move in partners while keeping all four feet firmly attached to the one spot.

- *Face your partner.*
- *You will need to work as a single unit for this, so find a way to attach yourselves together; i.e., join hands, join arms, put arms over shoulders.*
- *Make sure your feet are firmly on the floor, like they are glued to the ground. You cannot move them at all, not even a little bit. So wiggle around if you need to find a firm position.*
- *When I cue you, partners will move together in the ways I call out.*
- *Remember to stay attached and to stay glued to the floor. Only your bodies can move.*
- Provide movement cues.

Debrief: Discuss why this was difficult.

* * *

Sample Movements

- Trees in a storm
- A four-armed creature trying to reach something just out of reach
- Dancing: fast, slow, creative, ballet, country
- Marching or skating
- A four-armed creature trying to lift a big, heavy object

88. Sourpuss

Objective: To make your partner smile when she/he is trying not to.

- *Face your partner; be close but not touching.*
- *Decide who's S and who's F. We will change positions halfway through, so it doesn't matter which letter you are first.*
- *Partner F, you are Funny. When I give the Start cue, your job is to make S smile.*
- *Partner S, you are Sourpuss. Your job is to keep a straight face.*
- *Partner F, you can do anything but talk or touch your partner. This is a silent activity. And you must stay within the circle of your desks.*
- *Partner S, you have to remain a Sourpuss and not smile at your partner. As soon as S smiles, the round is over, and you have to switch positions.*
- Provide the Start cue. Watch students to decide when to change positions. Some students can keep a straight face forever; note these students for debriefing.

Debrief: Invite the students who do not smile to share their secrets of staying focused. Discuss when not smiling might be a good idea; e.g., when trying not to hurt another's feelings.

Sound and Movement

It's inevitable that, all moving at the same time, students will need to be reminded not to infringe on the space of others. Referring to the imaginary space that surrounds and encapsulates every student as a "personal space bubble" works well. Appreciation of the "bubbles" of peers seems to be a concept readily understood and accepted by all ages.

The 3-Minute Motivators in this section involve dynamic movements, often away from the desks, as well as verbal interactions. They turn students into controlled "movers and shakers." They all involve students working together; none are done on an individual basis. Although they often involve sound or speech, most don't require props.

At first glance it might seem that these refocusers are counterproductive, that they might create chaos rather than reduce it. This is not the case. Because the teacher is in control of the activity, and because actions are completely structured and directed, the ultimate goals of removing excess energy and/or reducing boredom are magically met.

In these activities, all strands of the Language Arts curriculum are covered, often by a single activity. Students are engaged in moving, demonstrating, listening, observing, copying, speaking, and, at times, reading and writing. These 3-Minute Motivators tend to make the best anticipatory sets (see page 12).

Students need to be reminded about personal space, respect for others, and safety issues. The following quick rules work well.

- Stay in your own bubble.
- Watch out for others, and don't puncture anyone else's bubble.
- Appreciate and respect what everyone is doing. No rights or wrongs.

Note:

- This is similar to Fast Feet (page 63) but differs in the forms of feet/leg actions.
- This activity is great to get endorphins flowing.

89. Going Noisily Nowhere

Objective: To engage in a brief physical yet stationary activity.

- *Stand beside your desk. We are going to really move.*
- *I will cue you to start moving, but you have to stay on one spot. You will be going nowhere—but getting there in some strange ways!*
- *Each way that you move can have an attached sound. For example, when marching you might want to go "Boom, boom, boom…" in time with your feet. Everyone will have a different sound. Or you might decide to have no sound. It's up to you.* Be prepared to demonstrate with sounds of your own as you lead the movements.
- Cue to start simply: *March slowly.* Speed up the march until it is quite fast, then change: *Hop with both feet together.*
- Keep changing the action, using any mixture of movements.
- Include a variety of alternating fast/slow movements that will use up excess energy in a positive way.
- You might want to invite students to call out ways to go nowhere themselves.

*   *   *

Sample Movements and Sounds

hop on one foot	"Click, click, click…"
jump with both feet on the floor	"La, la, la…"
wiggle the whole body	"Rum, rum, rum…"
walk in slow motion, as if in deep water	"Gurgle, gurgle, gurgle…"
march with stiff legs	"Bleep, bleep, bleep…"
crazy march, legs going in all directions	"Ribble, ribble, ribble…"
ragdoll walk, as if with no bones	"Slump, slump, slump…"

90. Ages of Humanity

Objective: To physically experience the aging of a human being, condensed into a few minutes.

- *For this game, you and your partner will be friends who start out life as babies and quickly "fast forward" to become old people.*
- *You will need to listen carefully to my side cues so you know what to do.*
- *Try to work together to really* feel *what happens to yourselves as you get older and older.*
- *You can use the area beside your combined desks, but do not interfere with the areas of others. Remember to respect the space bubbles of other pairs.*
- *Every time you hear my cue, you will grow older.*
- *With each new age you will say, "How are you? I am ___," to each other, filling in the last word appropriately. You must use the voice and words of that age.*
- *Listen carefully for my cue and freeze for a few seconds to hear the next directions.*
- *When I cue you to begin, you are both infants in cribs next to each other. You will have to lie on the floor to do this.*

- Cue to start. Continue at regular intervals with prompts, remembering to cue between ages. Wait until they speak after each cue.
  - *You are newborns. Look at each other. Kick your feet like babies and communicate with each other as babies in cribs might do.*
  - *Now you are babies. You are crawling on your hands and knees; you are starting to talk.*
  - *Now you are toddlers, just starting to walk. Lean on each other; take baby steps. Remember to stay in your space bubbles.*
  - *Now you are four years old, in playschool. Maybe you argue over a toy; maybe you share.*
  - *Now you are ten-year-olds. How do you behave? You are best friends.*
  - *Now you are teenagers. How do you look? Move? Talk? Carry on a conversation like typical teens.*
  - *Now you are young adults, still good friends. You have chosen careers—perhaps the same; perhaps different. Say your lines then discuss your jobs with each other. You are tall, confident, strong.*
  - *Now you are middle-aged—feeling a bit tired. How do you walk? Are you a bit overweight? Are you overworked? How do you feel? Say your lines then continue talking until I cue you.*
  - *Now you are very old, a grandparent. You use a cane to walk. You can't see or hear as well as before. Say your lines.*
  - *Finally, your ages of humanity are over. When I cue you, you will die peacefully by returning to the floor.*

Debrief: Quickly discuss how it felt to fast-forward the aging process.

Extended Debrief: Extended discussion and/or writing at another time.

Showcase: Invite any students to share a specific age.

Sound and Movement

Subjects: Language Arts; Phys Ed; Science

Individual

91. Move It

Objective: To return to desks, moving according to the teacher's directions.

- *When I give you the cue to move, you will walk as far away from your desk as possible, and then stand still. Remember to respect each other's personal spaces.*
- Cue to move away from desks.
- *Wait for the Start cue. You will return to your desks in an unusual manner. Follow the Move It suggestion as closely as possible.*
- *You can make any sounds you want to accompany the movements, but you cannot use actual words.*
- *Remember to respect the personal spaces (bubbles) of others while you are moving. If you accidentally bump another's space, find a way to apologize without using actually words.*
- If students are still restless, repeat the sequence, using a different Move It style.

Showcase: If a student comes up with a particularly creative move, suggest he or she demonstrate for all to enjoy.

＊　＊　＊

Move It Suggestions

- Like a spider/kangaroo/monster/snake/rabbit
- Through a thick jungle/forest/slough/rushing river
- On slippery ice/broken glass/hot cinders/rocky slope/deep snow
- Backward, sideways
- As if you are very old/are crippled/have broken leg/have only one leg
- Joined to someone else: back to back, hip to hip, elbow to elbow
- Leading with your shoulder, elbow, head, bottom, nose, little finger

---

Sound and Movement
Subjects: Any; Phys Ed
Partners

92. Walk This Way

Objective: To duplicate the walk and sound made by a leading partner, and to keep changing leaders.

- *Turn to your partner (neighbor, friend).*
- *When I give the Start cue, the two of you will stand, one in front of the other.*
- *When I give the cue again, the front person will start to walk and make some funny, not-too-loud sound.* Model a march or shuffle accompanied by a soft squeak with each step. *The leader must walk very consciously— thinking about each step, aware of where each foot goes.*
- *The person behind must copy the person in front.*
- *The two of you keep moving like that until you hear the cue again.*
- *Then you turn around and reverse positions. Now the other person leads, creating a different walk and sound.*
- *You must change leaders every time you hear the cue.*
- *You can move anywhere in the room, as long as you respect the personal spaces (bubbles) of others.*
- *Remember to keep your sounds soft, but creative. Try to use different styles of walking with each change.*

Debrief: Ask students what was funny or interesting about the refocuser.

Showcase: If any pair has demonstrated a particularly interesting walk/sound combination, ask if they would like to share with the class.

Sound and Movement

Subjects: Any; Phys Ed

Small Group

93. Wrangle Tangle

Objective: To tangle arms in groups of four or five, then move across the room while tangled.

- Quickly get students into small groups.
- *When I give the Start cue, you will stand in a small, tight circle. Cue.*
- *The goal here is to get tangled up. Reach in your right arm and join hands with someone else. You can tangle by going under someone's arm or turning around—whatever.*
- *You can talk quietly to each other during this refocuser.*
- *Now reach in your other arm and tangle up as much as possible.*
- *Now you are in tangled clumps. As a clump, you must think of a sound you will make together. You have ten seconds to come up with a clump sound.*
- *Making your clump sound, your tangled clump must move around the room for 30 seconds. If you meet another clump, figure out how to get around it.*
- Cue to start. Allow 30 (or more) seconds. Cue to stop.
- *Untangle—one step at a time—and return to your desks*

Debrief: Discuss the difficulty in moving as a clump. Are there situations in real life where this might happen (e.g., in crowds in subways, malls, airports; in mobs)?

Sound and Movement

Subject: Any

Whole Class

Props: An envelope; as many slips of paper as there are students

Prep: Mark several of the slips with an X; put all slips of paper in the envelope.

94. Explosion

Objective: To toss and catch an imaginary ball, and "explode" when a cue is provided.

- *For this game you will need to stand beside your desks.*
- *I will pass around this envelope. Take a slip, look at it, but keep it secret.*
- *Remember if there was an X on your paper. Hide the paper.*
- *Now I am going to call a name, and throw an imaginary ball to that person. That person must catch the ball, then call another person's name and throw the ball to him or her, and so on.*
- *If you had an X paper, shout "EXPLODE!" as soon as you catch the ball. Everyone has to make loud explosion sounds and fall to the floor.*
- *Stay frozen on the floor until I give the "Rise up" cue. Then the person who called "Explode" tosses the ball again.*
- *Remember, only some people can call "Explode." Once a person calls "Explode," he or she cannot call it again. So try to remember who has had the ball and who hasn't.*

Sound and Movement
Subject: Any
Whole Class

Note: Surprisingly, this refocuser works for any age. We all need to access our inner child at times, and to remember that there is a place for silly in every classroom.

95. The Old Duke Revisited

Objective: To stand and sit in increasingly rapid succession.

- This is a take off of the popular child's poem:

   The grand Old Duke of York, he had ten thousand men.
   He marched them **up** to the top of the hill and he marched them **down** again.
   And when they were **up**, they were **up**,
   And when they were **down**, they were **down**,
   And when they were only halfway **up,** they were neither **up** nor **down.**

- Students stand up or sit down when each of the **highlighted** words are sung, holding themselves halfway up on the last line, then standing, then sitting.
- Change the words according to the following example:

   Miss Manson's Grade 3 class were restless once again,
   So she marched them **up** to the top of the hill and she marched them **down** again.
   And when they were **up**, they were **up**,
   And when they were **down**, they were **down**,
   And when they were only **halfway up**, they were neither **up** nor **down**.

- *This is an action poem.*
- *First I say a line, then you repeat it.* Recite the entire poem without actions.
- *Now we move up or down on the* up *or* down *words. Let's try it slowly.* Practice at least once slowly.
- *Now more quickly!* Continue to increase the speed with each repetition.

Sound and Movement
Subject: Health & Wellness; Language Arts; Social Studies
Whole Class

96. Walk or Block

Objective: To move on cue, or to block on cue if movement is impossible.

- *Please move away from your desks to any spot in the room.*
- *When I give the Start cue, you are to move in exactly the way I say. For example, I might say, "Two forward," or "Two sideways."*
- *The number tells you how many steps to take. Each step is the size of your foot.*
- *The "forward" or sideways" tells you the direction to move.*
- *If you find you are stuck—facing a wall or desk and unable to move as directed—you turn into a "block." That means you can block others from moving by taking up as much space as you can, right where you are blocked.*
- *You cannot touch or grab—just be a still block.*
- Cue the movements. At some point most students will be blocked.

Debrief: Discuss how it felt to be blocked.

                                    *   *   *

Sample Movements

Any number, then

- Sideways, backward, diagonally, forward
- Any combination; e.g., two forward and one diagonally
- With the addition of other elements; e.g., eyes closed, arms in the air, legs stiff

---

Sound and Movement

Subjects: Health & Wellness; Language Arts; Social Studies

Whole Class

97. Meet and Greet

Objective: To walk around, greeting peers in as many unusual ways as possible.

- *When I give you the Start cue, your job will be to move freely around the room, greeting as many people as you can in two minutes.*
- *But there's a catch! You must find unusual ways to greet each other. You cannot rely on "Hi" and a wave. You must be creative.*
- *You might say "Yo!" or "Dude!" or even make up a nonsense word for hello.*
- *You might touch fists in greeting, or rub shoulders, or bow, or wiggle fingers. Be creative.*
- *You can keep changing the way you greet others, or stay with one way. You decide.*
- Cue to start, then watch for innovative greetings for showcasing.

Showcase: Invite students who greeted or responded to greetings creatively to share what they did.

Sound and Movement

Subjects: Health & Wellness; Music; Phys Ed

Individual as part of Whole Class

98. If You're Happy…

Objective: To participate in group exploration of the familiar tune "If You're Happy and You Know It."

- Review the song:

    If you're happy and you know it clap your hands (*clap clap*)
    If you're happy and you know it clap your hands (*clap clap*)
    If you're happy and you know it and you really want to show it.
    If you're happy and you know it clap your hands (*clap clap*)

- *We are not going to sing the song like that. We are going to change it.*
- *First we have to think of something else we might feel or do, instead of feeling happiness.* Invite suggestions.
- *Now we'll sing the song with our new ideas, and add appropriate actions.*
- *Once we've added a couple of verses, we'll start at the beginning with "happy" and put them all together.*
- Success of this motivator depends on quickly establishing other emotions or activities and associated actions.

*   *   *

Sample Emotions and Actions

• Angry	stomp your feet
• Tired	stretch your arms
• Lonely	hug yourself
• Restless	shake your hands
• Leaving	wave goodbye
• Frightened	rub your tummy

Sound and Movement

Subjects: Language Arts; Social Studies

Whole Class

99. Mad Milling

Objective: To move around the room in the personas of various characters.

- *When I give the Start cue, move to _____.* Indicate an open area of the room, or suggest moving carefully around furniture.
- *You will be milling. That means walking around, not touching anyone or interfering with their space.*
- *The fun is that you will be listening to my suggestions and walking according to them. You can also make any sounds that might accompany specific movements.*
- *For example, if I say, "Walk on hot coals," you might lift your feet quickly and say, "Ouch! Ouch!"*
- *When you hear the cue again, freeze and wait for the next suggestion.*

Extended Debrief: Challenge students to choose one form of movement and expand on it in writing; e.g., a story about a protagonist who moves that way.

Showcase: Invite students to demonstrate various movement strategies.

*   *   *

Sample Movements

Walking on
- Ice
- Broken glass
- Eggs
- Soft Fur

Walking as a
- Very old person
- Marionette
- Toy soldier
- Injured warrior
- Ninja

Walking through/in
- Deep water
- Mud
- Tall Grasses
- Snakes

Walking while feeling
- Tired
- Extremely happy
- Cold
- Afraid
- Sick

Sound and Movement

Subject: Art; Language Arts

Partners or Small Groups

Note: This refocuser provides great photo potential. As long as you have permission, try capturing the poses, printing and displaying them for future discussion, writing, or creative art.

100. Kodak Moments

Objective: To spontaneously create and hold perfect poses.

- Quickly get students into small groups of four or five.
- *You might have heard of a Kodak Moment. It means a picture-perfect moment, a time when people are perfectly posed to have their photo taken. Since we have phones in our cameras, we tend to take action shots; this is different. This is like posing for a photographer.*
- *You and your partner (group) will have 60 seconds to create and hold a perfect Kodak Moment.*
- *But here's where the fun comes in. I will tell you who you will be portraying before you arrange the pose.*
- *You can discuss the Kodak Moment with your partners, but you need to move very quickly. I'll tell you when the first 30 seconds is up.*
- *Let's see who can come up with the most creative poses.*
- *You will be working beside your desks (in the space at the back of the room, etc.). Remember not to move into the space of another pair (group).*
- *Once you have your pose, hold it—freeze it.*
- Begin cueing.

Extended Debrief: Challenge students to write (a story, a news article, a journal entry, etc.) about the people in the Kodak Moment, or do an Internet search for Kodak Moment pictures.

Showcase: Invite students to look around at the Kodak Moments of others before unfreezing them and/or moving to a new moment.

*   *   *

Sample Kodak Moments

- Family of teddy bears
- Group of superheroes
- Millionaire family
- Family of supermodels
- Family of hillbillies (or any geographically based group)
- Group of ballet dancers (or other kind of dancers)
- Group of preschoolers
- Group of angry criminals
- Group of nuns and priests
- Members of a team (soccer, basketball, football)
- Group of cartoon characters (each student picks favorite character)

Note:

- This refocuser encourages cooperation and divergent thinking.
- Allow students who don't like being touched to be judges of the effectiveness of the shapes. Or have each group include a Designer, who verbally guides the other group members.

101. The Shape You're In

Objective: To create specific shapes as members of a group.

- Quickly divide students into groups of four or five.
- *Listen carefully. When I give the Start cue, your group must work together to form a specific shape, using your bodies as one unit. For example, if I call "Circle," you could join hands. That's easy. But some of the shapes will be more difficult.*
- *You can talk quietly until your shape is ready, then you go silent.*
- *After a short time, I will cue to you stop. If your group isn't ready, it will be too late to work any more on that shape. So you'll need to work quickly.*
- Cue to Start and Stop according to how well students are doing with the task, and use as few/many of the shapes as needed to refocus.

Debrief: Discuss how easy/difficult this activity was and why. Discuss times in real life when we have to "be a part of a whole": e.g., team sports.

*   *   *

Sample Shapes

- Square, circle, triangle, rectangle, hexagram, pentagram
- Tree, house, boat, pyramid, car, train, plane
- Animal; e.g., elephant, kangaroo,
- Vehicle; e.g., truck, train, boat, jeep

Sound and Movement

Subjects: Language Arts; Science; Social Studies

Whole Class

Note: At first glance this refocuser might seem to appeal to only very young students. This is not the case; its success with all ages is guaranteed by the enthusiasm of the teacher. After all, everyone wants to belong and, at least at times, be a follower.

102. Pied Piper

Objective: To follow the leader.

- Have all students stand in a line. Randomly choose someone to be first in the line. Or choose to be the first Pied Piper yourself.
- *You have probably heard the story the Pied Piper. We're going to have fun with that idea.*
- *We are going to follow the Pied Piper around the room, doing exactly what he/she does and making any sound he/she makes.*
- *No touching each other. Just watch, listen, and mimic.*
- *Every few seconds I will give the Stop cue and you'll all freeze.*
- *Then I'll touch someone's shoulder and that person becomes the Pied Piper and moves to the front.*

*   *   *

Sample Movements

- Skipping, hopping, sliding, skating, marching (different tempos), baby steps (different tempos)
- Clapping, raising alternate arms, flying
- Arms crossed, straight out in front, held over heads
- Stiff legs, wobbly legs
- On knees, on hands and knees
- Changing levels: up high, down low
- Adding jingles or nonsense words to the movement; singing familiar tunes

Sound and Movement

Subjects: Language Arts; Math; Science; Social Studies

Partners or Small Groups

103. Blast Off!

Objective: To find ways to say and show "Blast off."

- Arrange students in partners or small groups of three or four.
- *Sit quietly with your partner/group and wait for directions.*
- *We have all heard the term "Blast off." It's usually the end of a countdown: …4, 3, 2, 1, Blast off!*
- *Your group must find a different way to say "Blast off." You will count down and change those two words; then you follow what your new term tells you to do.*
- *For example, if you decide to replace "Blast off" with "Hit the deck," you have to drop to the floor.*
- *The words and actions you come up with don't have to be a negative reaction. In other words, at the end of the countdown, you might shout, "Hug your neighbor." It can be anything you want to do at the end of a countdown.*
- *After I give the Start cue, you have two minutes to figure out what you will say and do. If you haven't come up with an idea at the end of the two minutes, just use the original "Blast off."*
- *At the end of planning time, we will count backward together. Each pair/group will say and do their new term at the same time.*
- Be sure to have all students count down together before they go into their individual pursuits. The final exhibition will be quite noisy and creative.

Debrief: This refocuser lends itself to discussions about expectations, and how we come to expect specific results from specific words or actions.

Showcase: This is great to use as a showcase by inviting each pair/group to demonstrate, if time allows.

*   *   *

Sample Alternatives to "Blast off"

- Hit the deck
- Fire in the hole
- Flatten to the floor
- Cover your head
- Dive down
- Hug your neighbor
- Do a dance
- Sit down gently
- Sing a song

104. Chain Spell

Objective: To spell a word that begins with the final letter of the previous word.

- *With this game, you can help each other be better spellers as well as quick thinkers.*
- *I am going to suggest a theme, then the first person in your pair/group will say a word related to that theme and spell it.*
- *Then the partner/next person has to think of a word, still on topic, that starts with the last letter of the preceding word. That person says the word and spells it.*
- *For example, if the theme is food, the first person might say "bread" and spell "b-r-e-a-d." The next person might say "donuts," because d is the last letter in* bread *and the first letter in* donuts.
- *This is not a competition, so make sure to help each other. See how many words you can cover in the time allotted.*
- Provide a theme based on current in-class study.

Sound and Movement

Subject: Language Arts

Whole Class

Props: Short selections of text for easy reading

Prep: Select reading text from any story or poem being read in class, or from any subject content, as long as the reading is relatively simple.

105. Beat Reading

Objective: To read short passages while following a specific rhythm.

- *We are going to have some fun with this short reading selection.* Indicate the selection and have students open to it.
- *I am going to set a beat by clapping, like this.* Set a steady clap rhythm.
- *Then I will ask for a volunteer to read to that rhythm, to "beat-read."*
- Model how this will work by saying one word with each beat. The sentence "The dog chased the cat" would be read, "The-dog-chased-the-cat."
- *Of course the fun will come when I change the beat. The reader has to change the way he or she is reading to match that beat.*
- Model again, using a different beat: with the beat slow–slow–quick–quick–quick, the sentence would be read, "The—dog—chasedthecat."
- Invite volunteers to read. If there are none, select readers, using the best readers first.
- *Remember that this is for fun, so let's clap for the readers and encourage them.*

Debrief: This is a good opening for a discussion about style of speaking, reading, singing.

* * *

Sample Beats

- Vary the tempo
- Vary the volume: soft beats, hard beats
- Clap hands, then slowly drag them apart: the word will be read with the end of it dragged out slowly
- Mix the tempos; e.g., slow–quick–slow–quick; quick–quick–quick–slow

Subjects: Language Arts; Science; Social Studies

Whole Class

106. Hummingbirds and Crows

Objective: To move and sound like hummingbirds and crows

- *Stand beside your desks.*
- *When I cue, you will all become hummingbirds. Hummingbirds move their wings very quickly and make little humming sounds.* Demonstrate, thumbs to shoulders, moving elbows up and down quickly, and humming. *Hummingbirds have to move their wings very quickly to appear motionless.*
- *When I cue you again, you will change into crows. Crows are big, noisy birds that go, "Caw, caw."* Demonstrate with arms wide out, making big, slow flapping movements, and harshly cawing.
- *You will keep changing from hummingbirds to crows with each cue. You can move away from your desk if you want to.*
- Cue the start and keep alternating birds every few seconds.

Sound and Movement

Subjects: Language Arts; Science; Social Studies

Whole Class

Note: Remind students they have the right to Pass, as they might not be comfortable with the attention that comes with leading.

107. Same Make, Same Model

Objective: To mime being robots and following a leader robot

- *Stand beside your desks. When I cue you to start, you will all become robots, and each of you will be identical to the Lead Robot.*
- *To begin, I'll be the Lead Robot. But I will touch people's shoulders, making them the Lead Robots.*
- *It will be up to the Lead Robot to move in a certain way and make a specific sound. Everyone else will have to copy exactly.*
- *Remember you are robots, not humans or other living beings. Be stiff, robotic.*
- Lead with typical robotic arm movements and a stiff walk for a few steps. Then choose another leader.

*   *   *

Sample Robot Movements and Sounds

- Slow head movements, trunk turns, bends
- Stopping between steps
- Lifting one knee and one arm together
- Straight-leg walking, marching, sliding
- Beeps, whirring sounds, *shhhh*s, pops

4

Let's Communicate

"The art of conversation is the art of hearing as well as of being heard."
— William Hazlitt, *Extended Essays, 1778–1830*

The 3-Minute Motivators in this chapter are communication-based motivators grouped as Single Words and Sounds, Conversations, and Brainstorming. In all three sections, students convey and/or interpret both verbal and nonverbal information. The sections differ in the complexity of the communication, as well as in the degree of divergent thinking required. All call for work as partners or teamwork; a few require paper and writing tools as props.

Single Words and Sounds

The motivators in this section require peer cooperation; in many cases students will be fast-talking in some manner with neighbors or nearby small groups. For the most part, these motivators involve individuals conversing or communicating within the protective confines of the entire group. Although individual students are completely independent, they are still part of a group, taking part in activities that culminate in magical minutes of sound making.

These motivators work well at times when students are fidgety but not focusing, when they are restless and not directing their thoughts to the lesson at hand—for example, following a video, story-reading, or Fine Arts class—or prior to a more-focused, cognitive task, such as writing or math work.

These motivators involve considerable cognition and creativity, as well as short-term memory. In addition, they encourage social constructivism, or learning from peers, which makes them excellent for diverse classrooms where some students may be less fluent with the language or less capable in communicative endeavors, and can benefit from peer interaction.

- In these activities, basic literacy skills come into play in an entertaining, motivating, and almost magical manner—plus talking is allowed and encouraged within the limitations of the activity. How much fun is that?
- Many of these 3-Minute Motivators benefit from debriefing.
- Many of the activities in this section lead beautifully into further individual tasks, such as writing or researching.

Single Words and Sounds

Subject: Any
Individual as part of Whole Class

Note: I have never had students continue talking after the Stop cue. They are so amazed that you invited them to talk that they readily adhere to the limits afterward.

108. Talk-a-lot

Objective: To talk non-stop about anything for a full 60 seconds.

- This activity works best when students have been excessively chatty, as it beats them at their own game.
- *It seems you all need some talk time. Okay, you have exactly one minute to talk.*
- *You must talk for a whole minute, but when I give the Stop cue, stop immediately and face me.*
- *Remember—everyone must talk when I say, "Go." Everyone will be talking at the same time. Get all you have to say said in one minute. You'll be surprised how long a minute can be.*
- *You have to talk sense—no nonsense or gibberish. Tell your partner everything you can think of.*
- *GO!*

Single Words and Sounds

Subjects: Any as source of words; Language Arts
Partners

Note: This refocuser is similar to Talk-a-lot, but uses gibberish instead of actual language; this one might be more effective than Talk-a-lot for younger students who have difficulty sustaining 60 seconds of talk.

109. Gibberish

Objective: To talk nonsense continuously for 120 seconds.

- *We all know what gibberish is—silly nonsense sounds that pretend to be words. Here's an example:* Offer a series of gibberish sounds; e.g., "ma-tha-nee-to-fa-ha-hooo."
- *When I give the Start cue, you will turn to your partner and say something in gibberish. Then your partner will talk back to you in gibberish.*
- *Try to carry on what seems like a logical conversation for two full minutes.*
- *Pay close attention to nonverbal communication—the body language that goes along with the gibberish. That can tell you a lot about what is being said even if the sounds are silly and nonsense.*
- Cue to start. Watch and listen for appropriate time to cue to stop.

Single Words and Sounds

Subject: Language Arts (phonetic awareness)
Individual as part of Whole Class

Props: Short reading selection

Prep: Choose a reading selection: part of a picture book, a piece of poetry, a section from a textbook or novel—whatever you wish; content is unimportant.

Note: This activity is a favorite with all ages. The word *Oscar* is an amusing and easy-to-say word that all ages enjoy shouting; however, any word can be used.

110. Oscar

Objective: To say "Oscar" every time a word or sound is heard.

- *Sit comfortably in your desks, feet on the floor, facing me. Don't slouch, because you will need to be very alert!*
- *I am going to read from _____ (name the text).*
- *Every time you hear the "s" sound at the beginning of a word (–ing ending; word that rhymes with at, etc.), you must shout out "OSCAR!"*
- Choose what the students are to listen for, considering ages, levels, and abilities of the students.
- If a word from a specific subject (e.g., *isosceles, equilateral, ecosystem, revolution*) needs reinforcing, use that instead of *Oscar*. To increase the difficulty, simply alter what the students must listen for: e.g., *Listen for any words related to ecosystems and shout "Ecosystem!" when you hear one.*

Single Words and Sounds

Subjects: Any as source of words; Language Arts

Individual

Notes:

- In addition to being a great refocuser, chanting activates our inner spiritual centres, making for more-focused students. It doesn't matter what is chanted, only that it is chanted in a sing-song, melodic manner. As you chant, your heart becomes lighter and your mood more positive.
- Choosing words from core curriculum (e.g., *equilateral*, *dinosaur*) is a way to reinforce vocabulary, spelling, phonetic awareness, and fun!

111. Interactive Words

Objective: To chant words as they are broken into pieces.

- Write a fairly lengthy word on the board, overhead, or interactive whiteboard.
- *Say after me.* Then lead them in a sing-song recitation of the different parts of the word.
- *This is a chanting activity.* Begin saying the word repeatedly, each time dropping a single letter from the beginning:

> *SPAGHETTI*
> *PAGHETTI*
> *AGHETTI*
> *GHETTI*
> *HETTI*
> *ETTI*
> *TTI*
> *TI*
> *I*

- Write other words and invite various students to lead the chant.

*   *   *

Sample Words to Chant

- *Everybody, shampoo, molasses, opportunity, communication, noisily, scrappy, nincompoop, grandmama, doodlebug*
- Students' names; e.g., *Tony* is chanted *Tony, Ony, Ny, Y*

Single Words and Sounds

Subject: Math

Individual as part of Whole Class

112. Count-Off

Objective: To attempt to count as high as possible, one student at a time.

- *Sit comfortably in your desks, feet on the floor, eyes front.*
- *You are going to count as high as possible as a class. Sounds easy doesn't it? How high do you think we can count?* Solicit responses.
- *But here's the tricky part. Anyone can say a number, but if two or more people say the number at the same time, we have to start all over.*
- *You can turn around so that you can see everyone, but remain in your desks. Watch and listen carefully so that no two people speak at the same time.*
- *No more than three seconds can go by between numbers.*
- *Start counting.*
- This is quite challenging. It's difficult to say a number without someone else saying it too. Most groups never get past 5 or 6.

Subject: Language Arts (phonetic awareness)

Individual as part of Whole Class

Note: Although this sound-blending game is suitable for young children, it works surprisingly well with older students too, especially if lengthy, interesting words are used. The suggestions below are divided by difficulty.

113. Hip-hip-hooray

Objective: To combine word parts into wholes and chant three times quickly, like a cheer.

- *This is a game where we all get to shout "Hip-hip-hooray," and throw our arms in the air. Let's try it once!*
- *Now circle one arm three times as if shouting "Hip-hip-hooray" or giving three cheers, such as "Rah! Rah! Rah!"* Model if necessary.
- *I am going to give you a long word, but I will say very slowly it all spread out. Like this: ca—ter—pil—lar.* Drag out the syllables and separate them completely so that students have to do the sound blending in their heads.
- *Quickly combine or blend the sounds in your head so that you know what the actual word is, then say the word itself three times like a cheer.*
- *When you've finished the three repetitions, shout "Hip-hip-hooray!" and throw your arms up!*
- *"Ca—ter—pil—lar" will sound like "CATERPILLAR! CATERPILLAR! CATERPILLAR! HIP-HIP-HOORAY!"*

Extended Debrief: If using this refocuser with older students, ask them to write down a couple of their favorite words and, when the interrupted lesson is complete, discuss what the words mean and use them in sentences.

* * *

Easier Words

Multiply	Banana	Paper	Winter
Family	Dinosaur	Happy	Butterfly
Communicate	Woman	City	
Alphabet	Kindergarten	Summer	

More-Difficult Words

Personification	Monologue	Serendipity	Trajectory
Appaloosa	Periodical	Misdemeanour	Precipitate
Conundrum	Onomatopoeia	Derogatory	Rigmarole
Cybernetics	Objectionable	Vestibule	Personification

Single Words and Sounds

Subjects: Health & Wellness; Language Arts

Individual as part of Whole Class

Props: Short phrases or poems

Prep: Select phrases suitable for chanting; post them where they are visible to all students.

Note: Chanting is known a form of relaxation. It is said to give confidence, joy, and satisfaction, and to build good karma—chanting in a classroom cannot be anything but good!

114. Chant-along

Objective: To chant simple words/text with peers.

- *Sit straight in your desk, feet on the floor, eyes on me.*
- *Don't lean against your chair back. Sit tall.*
- *We are going to chant together.*
- If students can read, put the chants on overheads or the interactive whiteboard. Otherwise, use the "I say, you say" method, and repeat the chant several times until memorization takes place.

Debrief: Invite students to suggest why chanting has a calming effect.

*　*　*

Sample Chants

1. Slowly I go, slowly I know, and slowly I grow—Slow! Slow! Slow!
2. I close my eyes, I close my ears. I say good-bye to hurts and fears.
3. The hurry in my head I cease, I fill it up with gentle peace. I close my eyes and beauty see. I deeply breathe, and calm I'll be.
4. One and two and three and four, I'm counting now, peace to restore. Five and six and seven too—relaxing, calming through and through.
5. *Pitter patter* falls the rain, making all seem clean again. Gently, softly falling down, in sparkling puddles all around.

Single Words and Sounds

Subject: Science

Individual as part of Whole Class

Note: As an alternative, you could invite each student to select his or her favorite animal then "sing" using the voice of that animal. Or students can "read" a short selection of text in animal voices.

115. Animal Farm

Objective: To participate, using animal sounds, in a whole-class animal chorus.

- *We are going to become an animal chorus.*
- Break the class into five or six equal parts (i.e., tables or rows), and assign each group one of the following animals: cows, chickens, ducks, horses, donkeys, pigs, dogs, cats.
- *First we need to practice the sounds these animals make.* Have each group, in unison, make the appropriate sounds.
- *You all know the tune _____.* Choose a familiar melody, such as "Three Blind Mice," "Twinkle, Twinkle, Little Star," "Jingle Bells," etc.
- *Now we will make our animal sounds to the melody; first one group at a time, and then all together.*
- Begin by having each group sing a line of the melody using the animal sounds; then have the entire group sing together.

Props: Sentences with punctuation missing (optional)

Prep: Select sentences; post on overhead/handout/interactive whiteboard

116. Punctuate This!

Objective: To become punctuation marks for a piece of text or reading.

- On the board, overhead, or interactive whiteboard, write a sentence containing a variety of punctuation: e.g., *The boy, his face red, shouted, "Where's my ball?"*
- As a class, identify all the punctuation marks.
- *We are going to BE the punctuation for this sentence. We will need sounds or actions that will represent each of the punctuation marks.*
- *Think about comic books where action words are written, like "Boom" or "Smash." We will be those action words for the different punctuation marks.* Demonstrate using an example, see below.
- *Now, each time we need one of these punctuation marks, you will* (make the sound, do the action).
- After a practice run, share sentences with the class, at whatever level the students are working. Encourage verbal and physical interaction with the punctuation marks.

> The boy (*squeak*) his face red (*squeak*) shouted (*squeak; click, click*) Where (*mmmmmm*)s my ball (*wooooo; click, click*).

*   *   *

Sample Punctuation Actions

- Period = clap once
- Comma = say "Squeak"
- Question mark = say "Woooooo" & make a swirl in the air with finger
- Quotation marks = two clicks of fingers
- Exclamation mark = shout "Bang!" & hit fist into hand
- Colon = say "Beep! Beep!"
- Semicolon = say "Beep, Ahhhhh"
- Apostrophe = say "Mmmmmmm"

117. Popcorn

Objective: To make tiny bouncing moves and popping sounds, like popcorn popping.

- *Sit tall in your seat and keep your feet on the floor at all times during this activity.*
- *You are going to be popcorn kernels in a popper.*
- *When I give the Start cue, start popping: bounce up a little on your chairs and make a light "pop" sound each time you bounce.*
- *We will bounce slowly at first—just like when popcorn starts off.*
- *Then we'll gradually get faster and louder as I cue you.*
- *As you pop, try to go from tiny kernel to puffy popcorn.*
- Side cue to increase speed and loudness.

Single Words & Sounds

Subjects: Any as source of theme topics; Language Arts; Math

Partners

118. Alphabet Pyramid

Objective: To think of words starting with subsequent letters of the alphabet.

- *Sit in your chair facing your partner.*
- *You will take turns speaking.*
- *I will give you something to talk about. You will say words connected to that theme, but every word you say must begin with the next letter of the alphabet in sequence.*
- *For example, you might start with "apple," then your partner would say "banana," then you could say "cake," and so on.*
- *Here's the catch—your words must build a pyramid. You use single words but you pile them up, pyramid style.*
- *So it would go "apple," "banana, banana," "cake, cake, cake," then maybe "donut, donut, donut, donut," and so on.*
- *All the words you say must fit the theme I give you. What theme was I using for the words I just shared?* (Foods)

*   *   *

Sample Themes

- School
- Summer holidays
- My favourite things
- Brothers or sisters
- Homework
- The forest/mountains, ocean/lake/river
- Any topic being studied in class

Single Words and Sounds

Subject: Math

Whole Class or Small Groups

Note: This can be simplified for younger students by using simpler conditions: every other person claps; every number with a 2 in it (not multiples of 2) e.g., 2, 12, 20, 22, etc.

119. Clap 3

Objective: To maintain an oral sequence of numbers, or counting, but to substitute a clap for every 3, number ending in 3, or multiple of 3. (i.e., For 3, 6, 9...or 30, 31, 32...or 43, 53, 63...)

- *This is a counting game. We will start at one side of the room and count the numbers in sequence. But here's the challenge! You mustn't say the number 3, or any multiple of 3 (6, 9, 12, etc.). Instead you must clap.*
- *For example, it would go like this: one, two, clap, four, five, clap, seven, eight, clap—and so on.*
- *Now here's where it gets really exciting. If a number even has a 3 in it, you must clap for the 3: For example, for 31 you must do this: Clap, one.*
- *There are no winners or losers here. We are working together to see how fast we can count.*

Single Words and Sounds

Subjects: Language Arts; Math
Partners

Note: Difficulty can be enhanced by placing a theme on the words; e.g., all words must have to do with a core subject unit of study. This works well as vocabulary reinforcement for a specific subject.

120. The Numbered Letter

Objective: To quickly think of a word starting with a specific letter.

- *For this game, I will start you off with a word and a number. You and your partner must say words that begin with a specific letter. But first you have to figure out what that letter is by counting letters in the supplied word.*
- *For example, if I say* school *and 3, you and your partner must say words that begin with the* **third** *letter in "school"—the letter* h.
- *The trick is to go as fast as you can. No repeating, no mumbling or hesitations.*
- *If one partner makes a mistake, then the other partner wins the first round. Just start again and keep going until I cue you to stop.*

Single Words and Sounds

Subject: Any
Individual as part of Whole Class

121. Quick Catch

Objective: To toss and catch an imaginary object.

- *For this game we will need to pay close attention to each other, because we are going to be throwing and catching an imaginary object to everyone in the class.*
- *You can decide in your own mind what the object is. It can be anything: a small ball, a football, a sword, a marble, a paper airplane, a heavy steel ball, a bowling ball, a pencil—whatever you can think of.*
- *Before you can toss your object, first you will need to catch whatever has been thrown to you. Make sure you make the movements to catch whatever the person says is being thrown to you. When you have caught the object, say, "Got it!"*
- *Then you must call the name of the person you are throwing to, and quickly say what you are throwing. For example: "Paul, catch the frisbee."*
- *The fun of the game is that we must work cooperatively. That means we have to try to remember who has already been thrown to, and throw to someone else until everyone has had a turn.*
- *Quietly think of what you might throw. Of course you can always throw a ball.*
- *I'll start. I am throwing an egg to _____ (name of student). He will have to catch it carefully, so as not to break it. When he has it he will say, "Got it!" Then he'll call a name and throw something different.*

Debrief: Quickly discuss what was easy or difficult to catch.

Conversation

Directed conversation can lead to critical thinking, innovation, and improved understanding.

For the 3-Minute Motivators this section, students work together, communicating by quickly responding to cues in order to carry on conversations in an unusual or controlled manner. In some cases, the conversations lead to a further activity, such as following a verbal direction with action. In all cases, the dialogues involve quick thinking, careful listening, organizational skills, and communication skills.

These motivators lends themselves to situations in which students need to focus on communication of all kinds—media, text, and visual, as well as culturally divergent communication forms, dialects, and languages. The tasks invite students to experiment with many varieties of communicative techniques in rapid, fun-filled, concentrated ways.

See page 14 for more on grouping students.

- These motivators make excellent starting points for all manner of journalling, follow-up writing, and discussing. In fact, many of them leave students with new insights into common everyday situations, as well as a variety of ideas for problem-solving. Quite naturally, these thoughts can become extended lessons.
- Since all these activities involve working with a partner, it might be a good idea to find ways to introduce variety in partners. Rather than always having students pair with the "the person next to you," try "every second person" or "person on the opposite side of the table or row." Just keep in mind that any movement to get to a partner can interfere with the three-minute time limit.
- Most of these refocusers do not require props or advance preparation.
- Most of these refocusers involve conversations, the topics of which will be provided by the teacher. Since nobody can always be creative and ingenious on the spot, I have provided a list of topics that could be used with any of the 3-Minute Motivators in this section.

Sample Topics
- Weekend activities
- Pet peeves
- Favorite animals, foods, sports, cartoon characters, people, places, etc.
- How you are feeling right now
- What makes you happy, angry, sad, excited, hopeful, frustrated, etc.
- Discussion of actions: a recently read story, an in-class activity, a field trip, etc.
- Discussion based on an in-class unit of study in any subject
- When you grow up…
- Your first experience with a doctor, dentist, school nurse, principal, etc.
- Theme-related topics; e.g., school, ecosystems, space, team sports, exercise, nutrition, video games, homework, sports, siblings, parents, clothing and fashion, technology (smart phones, computers, tablets, etc.)

Subjects: Language Arts; Music; Social Studies

Partners

Notes:
- Singing not only helps promote well-being in the classroom, but also settles and refocuses students.
- Even people who have difficulty with oral expression (e.g., stutterers) find that song helps them communicate more effectively.

122. Song Speak

Objective: To communicate only in song or melody.

- *Sit in your desk, facing your partner, feet on the floor and hands in your lap.*
- *The two of you are going to carry on a conversation entirely in song. You can communicate whatever you want, but you have to sing it.*
- *I will give you a topic to talk about.*
- *Remember to take turns "song speaking."*
- Model in song. Use a simple tune like "Three Blind Mice" if you don't feel creative. The following words fit the Three Blind Mice melody:

> *All of you,*
> *Yes, all of you,*
> *Will talk in song,*
> *In lovely, lovely song,*
> *About what you did last Saturday,*
> *Or maybe even Sunday.*
> *Song-speak about your weekend.*
> *Start singing now!*

Conversation

Subjects: Health & Wellness; Social Studies

Partners or Small Groups

Note: This refocuser addresses the core human trait of empathy; although it might not be fully developed, is often a first step toward compassionate action.

123. I Am You

Objective: To carry on a conversation "in the shoes of" a partner.

- If small groups can be readily formed, use them; otherwise, stick to partners for the sake of expediency.
- *You and your partner (group members) are going to carry out a discussion, but you must talk as if you actually ARE your partner.* Model by choosing two students:

  - *I am Bobby (Joan is speaking). I like playing hockey. I am good at it.*
  - *I am Joan (Bobby is speaking). I am good at school work.*
  - *(Joan speaking) Someday I will be a famous hockey star.*

- *I will give you something to talk about. You will discuss what you like and dislike, and maybe even what your pet peeves are, but no put downs—only positive comments. And remember you ARE the other person.*

Extended Debrief: This is a great activity to talk about at length at a later time. Discuss what it felt like having another person talk about you to your face, say good things about you, *be* you. Follow up with journalling about anything you learned about yourself.

124. Alphabet Speak

Objective: To carry on a conversation in which each sentence begins with the next letter of the alphabet.

- *You need your alphabets for this game.* Refer students to individual alphabets or alphabet on wall. With older students, memory of the alphabet is all that's necessary.
- *I am going to tell you what to talk about, then you and your partner (group) will discuss the topic. Each person must say a complete sentence. The FIRST word of that sentence will begin with whatever letter comes next in the alphabet. For example, on the theme of Homework:*

    A lot of kids hate homework
    But I am not one of those kids.
    Can you tell me why?
    Don't know!
    Every time I get homework, I hate it.

- *If someone can't think of a sentence in a few seconds, that person is out. One of you could end up a winner, or you could both (all) get completely through the alphabet.*
- *Here is your topic.* Choose a topic or use one suggested on page 98.
- The challenge aspect (competition between players) can be omitted and the game can be entirely cooperative. For younger children, just saying words according to a theme, or making the conversation themeless, can simplify the game.

Showcase: It can be a lot of fun if two students want to face-off before the entire class and attempt the game for all to hear and enjoy. A good choice of themes helps to keep the situation amusing.

125. Slow-Mo

Objective: To carry on a discussion that continually switches from fast speaking to slow motion.

- *This is a talking game.*
- *You and your partner will talk about a topic that I will provide.*
- *The catch is that you must talk either very quickly—as if someone has put you on fast forward—or very slowly in s-l-o-w m-o-t-i-o-n.*
- *You will change from one to the other every time you hear my cue.*
- *It doesn't matter who is talking when you hear the cue. Just continue the conversation, but change the speed.*
- *Remember—in any good conversation, both people get a chance to speak.*
- Give topic (see page 98 for suggestions) and cue to begin.
- Cue to change speeds every few seconds.

Showcase: Invite students to share a short dialogue, just for the entertainment value.

126. A Quantity of Questions

Objective: To carry on a conversation, based on a specific theme, using questions only.

- *Turn to face your partner.*
- *You are going to carry on a conversation about _____. Give topic (see page 98 for suggestions).*
- *But the catch is you must speak in questions. For example, if I was talking to my partner about school, the conversation might go like this:*

  Do you like school?
  Do you?
  I think you do, don't you?
  Do you think our teacher is good?
  Are you asking me if I like our teacher?

- *Remember to use only questions. If one of you forgets to use a question, you are both out. Let's see how long you and your partner can last. You need to help each other.*

Debrief: Invite students to share what was difficult about this.

127. You Did What?

Objective: To quickly and spontaneously share with a group three or four sentences about a nonsensical, teacher-supplied topic.

- Quickly get students into groups of four or five, sitting in small circles.
- *I will give you a silly topic, called a "lead statement." Every lead statement will begin with "What did you do when…"*
- *We will move around the circle, and each person will say the first thing that comes to mind about the topic. For example, if the lead statement is, "What did you do when you woke up in the middle of the jungle?" I might say, "I first started to scream. But when I saw some monkeys swinging through the trees, I decided to join them."*
- *Decide who will speak first; that person raises his or her hand to show me.*
- *I might use my Stop cue to change the topic before it gets around the circle.*
- *If anyone wants to use the Pass on a turn for one time around, that's okay. But no more than one Pass per person.*

*   *   *

Sample Lead Statements

What did you do when…
…your pet started talking to you?
…you landed on the moon in your newly built space shuttle?
…you opened your closet to find Homer Simpson (or Brad Pitt, or Justin Bieber)?
…you looked in the mirror and had no reflection?
…you ate a cookie and suddenly found yourself shrinking?
…you suddenly had the ability to fly (or other superhero power)?

Prep: Distribute People Who…
sentence starters as a handouts,
or post on a chart, the board, the
interactive whiteboard.

Note: This refocuser deals indirectly
with the issue of stereotyping.;
however, it can just as easily be
used for comedic value.

128. People Who…

Objective: To complete open-ended sentences related to behaviors of people.

- *With your partner, you are going to end some sentences in any way you want to.*
- *There are no right or wrong endings; whatever comes to your mind is good.*
- *Write down your endings and we will share later.*
- Cue to begin, and later to stop.
- Adjust the length of time for this refocuser according to how many sentence beginnings you provide. A good rule of thumb is one minute per sentence. Encourage spontaneity.
- Share some responses.

* * *

Sentence Starters

People who…

- park in others' driveways
- volunteer
- shout in public
- watch TV all day
- climb mountains
- smoke in public
- toss litter out of car windows
- go to the opera
- are noisy in a theatre
- don't pay taxes
- teach school
- work out regularly at clubs or gyms
- spend too much money
- drive trucks

Conversation
Subject: Any
Partners

129. You DON'T Say!

Objective: To carry on a conversation without ever using specific words.

- *This game is a talking game. You must carry on a conversation with your partner, but you cannot use some specific words.*
- *You cannot use "AND" or "I" for this conversation. For example, if I wanted to say "Last night I stayed home and did homework," I'd have to say, "Last night this person stayed home. This person did homework."*
- *If someone uses "and" or "I," that person is out and the other is the winner.*
- *If one of you gets out, you can start again if there's time left.*
- *I will tell you what to talk about and what words you cannot use.*
- *Begin when I give the Start cue.*
- Give topic (see page 98 for suggestions) and word(s) to eliminate. Cue to start.

Debrief: Quickly discuss how difficult it is to exclude particular small words from dialogue.

* * *

Sample Words to Eliminate

- The
- And
- I
- He/She
- My
- But

Subjects: Health & Wellness; Language Arts

Partners

130. "Yes, But" Pet Peeves

Objective: To carry on an escalating conversation about pet peeves, in which each speaker has a worse peeve than the previous one.

- *Sit facing your partner.*
- *You are to carry on a back-and-forth conversation for a full two minutes.*
- *You must each start what you say with, "Yes, but…" For example, if the starter is "The stars are pretty," the first person might say, "Yes, but they are far away." Then the next person might say, "Yes, but they look closer with a telescope," and so on.*
- *I will tell you what to talk about and provide the opening sentence.*
- Provide theme and cue to start.

Extended Debrief: *When do we use "Yes, but…" in day-to-day talk? When we use "Yes, but…," what are we saying or doing to what the other person said? (We are negating it.)*

        * * *

Sample Starters

- School is really tough.
- I forgot my lunch today.
- It's raining and we can't have recess.
- My dog ran away.
- My mom has to go to work.
- I spent all my allowance on candy.
- My dad got a new car.

Conversation

Subject: Health & Wellness

Partners

Notes:
- This refocuser gives students a way to acknowledge the goodness in their lives and, we hope, to realize that the source of at least some of that goodness lies outside themselves. It can be a cathartic experience, even when used as a 3-Minute Motivator.
- Alternative beginnings for this refocuser include *I appreciate…, I am grateful for…, I treasure….*

131. Glad Game

Objective: To carry on a conversation in which partners complete the sentence beginning "I am glad…"

- *Sit facing your partner.*
- *You are to carry on a back-and-forth conversation for a full two minutes.*
- *You must each start what you say with "I am glad…" For example, I might say, "I am glad I am here today," and my partner might say, "I am glad I have my homework done."*
- *Don't react to your partner's comment. Just follow it with a glad statement of your own.*
- *What one person says doesn't have to relate to what the other says; you simply have to keep thinking of what you are glad for or about.*
- *You must keep talking until I stop you.*

Extended Debrief: Invite students to recall as many things as they can that they said they were glad about, and to list them in their journals. Have each student select one to write about further.

132. Fortunately/Unfortunately

Objective: To converse with a partner when one person always begins with "Fortunately," while the other begins with "Unfortunately."

- *Sit facing your partner.*
- *Decide who is A and who is B.*
- *You are to carry on a back-and-forth conversation for a full two minutes.*
- *You must start what you say with "Fortunately" or "Unfortunately."*
- *Partner B will start and begin all sentences with "Fortunately." Partner A will begin all sentences with "Unfortunately." For example, B might say, "Fortunately today is Friday." Then A could respond, "Unfortunately we have homework for the weekend."*
- *When I cue to switch, you will start your sentences with the opposite word.*
- Cue to start. Continue for about one minute, then switch roles.

Debrief: Ask students if they learned anything. There can always be a "fortunate" or an "unfortunate," depending on our outlook.

Extended Debrief: Invite students to create comparison charts for which they think of opposing "fortunates" for any "unfortunates" they might have.

Conversation

Subjects: Health & Wellness; Social Studies
Partners

Props: Slips of paper, as many as there are students; a container for slips to be drawn from.

Notes:
- This works best with partners, as sometimes a single student can't think of an appreciation for the specific student(s) drawn.
- When we show appreciation, we not only make the other person feel important, but we also enhance relationships and give ourselves a boost as well. Appreciation is free, but very valuable.

133. I Appreciate…Because

Objective: To state an appreciation of peers.

- *First I need you to print your name on the small paper I hand out. Fold the paper once, then put it in the container.*
- *Sit comfortably facing your partner (neighbor, friend).*
- *I am going to randomly draw two names and hand them to each partnership. If you draw the name of a member of the pair, draw again, so every pair has names that are not their own.*
- *I will give you 30 seconds to think of a reason you appreciate each of the students whose names have been given to you.* Provide 30 seconds. If any students come up with nothing, be prepared to prompt with suggestions.
- *When I give the Start cue, you will take turns saying "I appreciate…" and completing the sentence. One partner says one name and appreciation, and then the other partner has a turn.*
- Demonstrate: *I appreciate (name of peer teacher) because he always…*
- Point out that the appreciation can be for physical, emotional, mental, or personality traits.
- Let each student speak before debriefing the refocuser.

Debrief: Discuss how if feels to be appreciated (or unappreciated)

* * *

Sample Prompts

- Physical abilities: strength, fitness, specific skills/abilities, good sportsmanship
- Mental abilities (personality): intelligence, wit, sense of humor, patience, compassion

- Friendship traits (personality): reliability, honesty, dependability, trustworthiness
- Things that person has done for you or others: e.g., helped clean up; played with the little kids at recess; shared lunch with _____.
- Comments that person has made: e.g., told _____ he/she did a good job; said she liked my _____

Conversation

Subject: Any

Partners

Note: This refocuser encourages wishful thinking, or imagining the best possible outcome or scenario without thought to reality or fact. But what begins as a wishful daydream can be turned into reality with the power of positive thinking, which is vital for achieving success.

134. May There Be...

Objective: To discuss possibilities.

- *This is a game of imagining and wishing.*
- *All you have to do is take turns completing the sentence starters: "May there be…" or "May there never be…"*
- *In partners, decide who's A and who's B.*
- *Partner B, you will start with "May there be…"*
- *Partner A, you will say "May there never be…"*
- *You will continue this for three sentences each; that is six sentences altogether. Then you'll switch and Partner A will start with "May there be…"*
- *What kinds of things might you say? How about "May there be sunshine today"? "May there never be a tornado here"? It can be something out of your control—just let your imaginations go.*
- *At the end of the talk time, we'll try to recall some of the ideas.*
- Cue to start. If necessary, provide a starting sentence.
- Stop after a couple of minutes, or when students get bogged down.

Debrief: Discuss the differences between wishful thinking that is out of our control and things within our control.

Extended Debrief: Explore the possibility of writing poems based on the ideas students have generated.

*   *   *

Sample Starting Sentences

- May there be enough for everyone to eat.
- May there be good weather for the track meet.
- May there be no homework tonight.
- May there be no more fights at recess.
- May there be no substitute teachers for (subject).

135. Third-Person Talk

Objective: To carry on a discussion in third person.

- *This is a curious game of communication.*
- *You have to talk to your partner about something you will do or have done, BUT you have to speak about yourself in third person.*
- *In other words, instead of saying "I did…," I would need to say "(Your name) did…" Instead of saying "give it to me," I would say "give it to (your name)."*
- *This is harder than it sounds.*
- *I will give you a topic to discuss. (See page 98 for suggestions.) When I give the Start cue, you must talk for two full minutes in third person.*

Debrief: Quickly discuss what was difficult, and when such a manner of speech might be used.

Extended Debrief: Challenge students to write a story in third person.

Showcase: Invite any pair who seem "natural" at this to share a brief discourse with the class.

136. Hi-Lo Speak

Objective: To place yourself physically higher or lower than a partner when speaking.

- *In this game, the person who is talking must always be HIGHER up than the listener. For example, if I am talking with Ruth, when I talk, I must raise myself much higher than Ruth. But when she speaks, even if it's just to say "Yes" or "No," she must be higher than I am.*
- *The idea is that the speaker is always looking down at the listener.*
- *To make it really fun, each person should not talk for long. The shorter your sentence or reply, the more quickly the two of you will have to adjust your positions.*
- *You will work together; you need to move down when your partner is speaking to allow him or her to move up.*
- *Think of what would happen in a Yes–No–Yes–No argument. You'd be bouncing up and down rapidly.*
- *When I give the cue, you will begin talking about the subject I will provide, and continue until I cue you to stop.*
- Provide topic (see page 98 for suggestions) and cue to start.

Debrief: Quickly discuss what was fun or difficult about this.

Extended Debrief: With older students, this lends itself to more in-depth discussions about being metaphorically higher or lower than others.

Conversation

Subjects: Health & Wellness; Language Arts

Partners

Note: This 3-Minute Motivator is especially good for times when students have been complaining or whining about something.

137. Poor Me!

Objective: To exaggerate feeling sorry for oneself.

- *For this game we get to really feel sorry for ourselves.*
- *Turn to face your partner.*
- *One partner starts by saying something that is troubling him/her, starting with, "Poor me,…." For example, "Poor me, I have to go to the dentist after school."*
- *The other partner has to "one up" that Poor Me by saying something even more self-pitying.*
- *Remember, you can say anything, but it has to be based on truth. Just feel really, really sorry for yourself and feel free to exaggerate the truth.*
- Cue to start.

Debrief: Ask if any students want to share their absolute worst Poor Me. Discuss how easy it is to get into catastrophizing and feeling overly sorry for ourselves, and how it can even become comical.

Conversation

Subject: Any

Partners or Small Groups

Props: Paper and a writing tool per student

138. I Am!

Objective: To share five self-descriptive words with a partner or group.

- *Listen…who are you? Silly question? Not really.*
- *I want you to think of yourself and jot down the first five words you think of that describe you.*
- *Use single words only. For example, for myself I would write "conscientious."*
- Give Start cue and allow no more than two minutes.
- Invite students to share one or more of their words with partners or groups.

Debrief: Discuss why we sometimes don't know exactly who or what we are, and how we can learn more about ourselves.

Extended Debrief: Use the lists to write personal essays or narratives.

Brainstorming

These 3-Minute Motivators beautifully and quickly reinforce skills of collaboration and improvisation. While most are designed for teamwork, as brainstorming is intended to leverage the collective thinking of the group, some work well as partner activities too. The refocusers here are socially constructive in nature and cover all strands of the Language Arts curriculum. Students will work together to quickly generate ideas based on teacher guidelines and suggestions. They might be jotting these ideas on paper, reading them, and sharing them, all in rapid succession. In fact, because these motivators are carried out under time pressure, and because they are generally competitive in nature, they become quite heart-thumping experiences. Positive competition is highly motivating and not to be discouraged in the refocusers of this section.

These activities engage students in imaginative thought, quick thinking, and rapid recall of information. They are both cognitive and stimulating in nature. Consequently, they are great for revving up sleepy brains, for jump starting lethargic imaginations, and for generally engrossing students in an exciting and challenging manner, so that students return to an interrupted topic with renewed vigor.

Some of these refocusers might seem similar to those in the Conversation section; the difference lies in the fact that they require more innovative and divergent off-the-wall, out-of-the-box thinking. As with all brainstorming activities, brains will be full speed ahead.

- Debriefing and extended debriefing can be valuable for the activities in this section, as many of them can be expanded into worthwhile writing, research, or discussion topics.
- Since many of these activities are timed challenges between groups, prizes definitely enhance the fun element. The mere idea of a prize can elevate students' level of commitment. See page 19 for prize suggestions.

Brainstorm
Subject: Language Arts
Small Groups

139. Times-10 Tales

Objective: To cooperatively create a ten-sentence story, complete with protagonist, plot, climax, etc.

- *Sit with your group members.*
- *Together you are going to create a story about _____.* Provide theme (see page 98 for suggestions).
- *But here's the catch. You must use exactly ten sentences!*
- *And you have to remember the story in your head—no writing.*
- *There are three/four of you in each group, so you have to take turns. Each group member will provide one or two sentences to make your tale.*
- *The story must make sense. Think of all the things that make a good story and be sure to get them all into exactly ten sentences.*
- *You will have two minutes to complete your story, so you'll have to work quickly.*
- *Choose one person who will be the tale-teller to convey the story to the rest of the class.*
- Cue to start.
- After two minutes (or more, if desired), cue to stop and allow the stories to be shared.

Debrief: Discuss story parts as related to story writing.

Extended Debrief: Invite students to write out their stories, moving away from the ten-sentence rule and embellishing the bare facts so that each group member's story turns out a little different.

Showcase: Invite individuals to share their stories.

Brainstorm

Subjects: Language Arts; Social Studies

Partners or Small Groups

Props: Point-of-view cards

Prep: Make cards with the point-of-view starters, so they can be reused

140. Point Please?

Objective: To look at a familiar situation from different points of view.

- *For this game you will need to think in unusual ways, but also think quickly and brainstorm together.*
- *I will give you a situation that is familiar to all of us; for example, a rainy day.*
- *Your job is to think of as many different ways as possible to look at or think of a rainy day. For example:*

  - *A disappointment for kids going on a picnic*
  - *Great for farmers in a drought*
  - *Good for fish or ducks*
  - *Bad news for people living near a high river*

- *This will be a competition. The group with the most points of view will win.*
- Draw a point-of-view card. Cue to start.
- Don't allow students more than about two minutes. Keep it snappy.
- Cue to stop.

Debrief: Tally to find a winning partnership or group, then share those viewpoints with the class.

Extended Debrief: Transfer the idea of different viewpoints to literature (e.g., point of view of a character) or to other subjects (e.g., Social Studies: point of view of displaced persons), and discuss. Or challenge students to write from an unfamiliar point of view.

*   *   *

Sample Points of View

- Being a victim of a natural disaster: forest fire, flood, earthquake, storm
- Losing something of value: wallet, ID, pet, sentimental jewelry
- Being a story protagonist who steals from the antagonist
- Being stranded on a very hot day on the desert
- Having the family car break down on holidays
- Being injured in an accident and ending up in hospital
- Being "dumped" by your boyfriend/girlfriend (adolescents love this one)
- Being the brunt of bullying/bad jokes/teasing
- Seeing a group of kids throwing rocks at an animal

Brainstorm

Subject: Language Arts
Small Groups

Note: This game might be too difficult for children younger than about eight.

141. And the Real Meaning Is...

Objective: To brainstorm as many original and humorous meanings of common words as possible.

- *For this game I am going to give you a common word; you and your partner are to brainstorm as many different ways to describe the meaning as you can. For example, if the word is "lazy," you might say*

  People who leave their clothes on all night so they don't have to dress in the morning
  A person who lies on top of the bed so he doesn't have to make the bed
  Someone who eats soup out of the can so she doesn't have to wash a pot

- *You will need to be really creative, maybe even silly.*
- *Remember, you aren't actually giving the definition of the word. You are explaining what the word means when it is used to describe someone or something.*
- *I will give you two minutes to brainstorm ideas and jot them down if you want to.*
- *We will share some of the ideas*

Extended Debrief: Use the brainstormed ideas as writing projects, working them into a story or character description.

Showcase: Share a few examples by mounting them or displaying them so that all can enjoy.

*   *   *

Sample Words

- happy
- workaholic
- tired
- famous
- bored

- compulsive
- evil
- brave
- silly
- good-hearted

- generous
- predictable
- smart
- witty
- cunning

Brainstorm

Subject: Any; Language Arts
Partners or Small Groups

Props: Pencil and paper

142. Synonym Sense

Objective: To quickly brainstorm synonyms for common words.

- Pair students or divide class into groups of three or four.
- *I am going to provide a word, and you are to brainstorm together to think of as many other words as you can that mean the same, or almost the same, thing. You will jot down all the words you come up with.*
- *You will have 30 seconds per word.*
- *This is a competition: after two minutes (that is, four words), I will compare your lists to find the winning pair/group!*
- It's a good idea to do a quick one together as a model: *For the word "say," I would write* speak, utter, talk, chat, verbalize, lecture, address, tell, cry, announce, exclaim, reply, shout, *etc.*
- Give the first word. After 30 seconds, cue with the second word; and so on for four words. Cue to stop.

*   *   *

Sample Words with Many Synonyms

- look
- fat
- thin
- big
- small

- pretty
- ugly
- run
- move quickly
- move slowly

- think
- say
- look

Brainstorm

Subject: Any as source of combinations

Small Groups

Props: Writing tools and paper

Note: This can be a competition if you like, but it is not necessary. The challenge is inherent.

143. Go-Togethers

Objective: To quickly think of things that go together.

- *I am going to say the first part of a phrase you are familiar with: "fish and …" What part have I left out? Shout it out. "Chips!"*
- Here are a few more to practice with:

  brothers and…
  cats and…
  peaches and…

- Divide class into small groups. Make sure each group has a pencil and paper.
- *Your group is to quickly think of what could have been left off and write it down. See how many you can get.*

*   *   *

There may be appropriate responses other than the ones offered in parentheses. These are just guidelines.

Mathematics Phrases

- add and (subtract)
- multiply and (divide)
- positive and (negative)

- problem and (solution)
- height and (weight)

General Phrases

- peanut butter and (jam)
- pancakes and (syrup)
- cake and (ice cream)
- bread and (butter)
- mothers and (fathers)
- dads and (moms)
- sisters and (brothers)

- grandmothers and (grandfathers)
- keys and (locks)
- shoes and (socks)
- in and (out)
- up and (down)
- north and (south)
- east and (west)

Brainstorm

Subject: Any as source of words; Language Arts

Partners or Small Groups

Notes:

- A good idea is to use content from a current topic in a subject, such as "ecosystems" from Science.
- An alternative is to change Word Tennis to Word Association. The students say whatever the previous word makes them think of. For example, "snow" might lead to "white," to "black," to "witch," and so on. This tends to be a bit more difficult, but equally entertaining and thought-provoking.

144. Word Tennis

Objective: To "toss" words rapidly back and forth between partners or group members.

- *Sit facing your partner (the members of your group).*
- *This is a quick-thinking talking game.*
- *I will give you a theme—a big idea—and all the words you say must fit into this theme. For example, if the theme is* Food, *then you could say, "eggs, bread, ice cream…."*
- *The idea is to say a word as quickly as possible. You can't wait more than three seconds or you are out.*
- *If you repeat a word, or say "ah" or "um," you are out.*
- *You will go back and forth between partners (in turn around the group).*
- Provide a theme and watch the fun.
- As you note several pairs/groups finish (i.e., run out of ideas) stop the game and provide another theme.

Showcase: An entertaining quick conclusion to this activity is to invite any two students to face-off and attempt the game with the class watching.

Brainstorm

Subjects: Language Arts

Small Groups

Props: Writing tools and paper

Note: This refocuser is a take-off of the popular Transformers movies, games, and toys. You might wish to introduce it by calling attention to any/all of these.

145. Transform It

Objective: To generate ways or transforming or changing common items.

- *We are going to have fun by thinking of different ways to transform, or change, some common items by coming up with different uses for them.*
- *I will suggest the items. For 60 seconds, your group will brainstorm all the uses—silly, imaginary, funny—for that item. In this way you will transform the item.*
- You might want to give an example: *My coffee cup could be transformed into a hat for a monkey, or a vase, or a pencil holder. Try to give both possible and impossible transformations in your example to encourage divergent thinking.*
- Provide an object and cue to begin. Watch to see when to give another word or stop the refocuser.

* * *

Sample Items to Transform

- pencil
- scissors
- ruler
- coffee cup
- paper clip
- interactive whiteboard
- overhead projector
- waste-paper basket
- cell phone
- computer screen
- seats or chairs

Brainstorm

Subjects: Health & Wellness; Language Arts

Partners or Small Groups

Props: Writing tools and paper

Note: This 3-Minute Motivator is based on positive thinking techniques and is great to use when spirits are down.

146. Rephrase/Reframe/Refresh

Objective: To change negative thinking into positive thinking

- *You will work together to take a situation and change it by*

    1. *rephrasing it or rewording it*
    2. *then reframing it, thinking of a more positive way to say it*
    3. *then refreshing it by discussing how the new wording is better than the original*

- *For example, if I give you the situation "The weather today is dark and gloomy," you could rephrase it as "The weather is rainy"; reframe it as "But the grass will look great"; and refresh by seeing that appreciating the weather is a better outlook.*
- *Use paper and pencil to write down your work.*
- Cue to begin and watch for the best time to cue to stop. You can leave the refocuser at this point—the very action of the motivator, without discussion, is uplifting—or you can debrief.

Debrief: Discuss how this refocuser could be put to use in daily life.

Brainstorm

Subject: Any

Whole Class

Props: Writing tool and paper for teacher

Note: This is the only whole-class refocuser in this section, but it can be done in small groups too.

147. Mystery Word

Objective: To determine a mystery word by asking yes/no questions.

- *This is a game for which the prize is guessing the mystery word.*
- *I have written a word on this paper.*
- *Your job is to guess this word by asking yes/no questions.*
- *You can ask only one question. Then someone else has to ask a question.*
- *The first person (partnership/group) to guess the word wins!*
- Invite questions. If students are slow to get going, give hints such as, "It's alive," or "It's in this room."
- Use any word(s) at all—even content-specific vocabulary.

Brainstorm

Subject: Any

Small Groups

Props: One piece of paper and one writing tool per group

148. Quick Questions

Objective: To brainstorm as many questions as possible for a teacher-presented answer (based on the popular TV show *Jeopardy*).

- *I am going to give you a statement that will serve as an answer.*
- *Each group has to think of and write down as many questions as possible for that answer, in a very short length of time.*
- *For example, if the answer is "The ocean," questions might be "Where do whales live?" or "What is a large body of water called?"*
- Provide an answer and cue to start.
- Keep the pace quick, and compare the number of appropriate questions for each answer.

Brainstorm

Subject: Any

Small Groups

Props: One piece of paper and one writing tool per group

149. Under the Umbrella

Objective: To generate items/characters that can fit "under" a specific cue

- *This game is called Under the Umbrella, and your job is to think of everything that could possibly go there—under the umbrella, or under whatever thing I give you.*
- *Choose a recorder for your group. That person has the paper and writing tool, and will jot down all your ideas.*
- *See how many things you can think of that could go under the item I tell you.*
- *Work together. You can be as silly and creative as you want to.*
- Announce the first umbrella word. Cue to start and watch for signs that it is time to cue to stop. You can do two or three "unders," then compare responses if desired.

* * *

Sample Umbrella Words

Under the…

- thimble, cup, teaspoon, handkerchief
- mushroom, flower, blade of grass
- cloud, rainbow,
- car, train, boat
- ocean, dessert, mountain
- rock, log
- house, floor, roof, blanket, bed, carpet

Brainstorm

Subject: Language Arts

Partners

Props: One piece of paper per partnership; a writing tool per student

Note: For a simplified version of this game, provide a list of small words and invite partners to brainstorm for bigger words within a time limit. If competition is desired, the pair with the most big words wins.

150. Big Word/Small Word

Objective: To quickly morph small words into bigger words.

- *Sit facing your partner (neighbor, friend).*
- *Partner A will say a small word, like "cat."*
- *Partner B has to think of a bigger word that has "cat" in it, like "caterpillar."*
- *As soon as Partner B has the bigger word, B gives A a small word to morph into a big word.*
- *Keep a list of your big and small words as you go.*

* * *

Sample Small Words

- in
- at
- or
- if
- ill
- got
- dog
- ring
- see
- eat
- do
- but
- with
- ate
- call
- able
- all
- par
- no

Brainstorm

Subject: Any

Small Groups

Props: One piece of paper per group; a writing tool per student

151. Excuses, Excuses

Objective: To brainstorm more excuses than any other group in a set length of time.

- *This is a great game at which you are all very good.*
- *Sit facing the other members of your group.*
- *When I give the Start cue, your group will brainstorm as many excuses as you can for the situation I will provide.*
- *Jot down your excuses. We'll share some of them later.*
- *Be creative. The excuses can be as wild or silly as you want.*
- *Provide a situation and cue to start.*

Extended Debrief: Invite students to choose one very unusual excuse (their own or someone else's) and elaborate it into a story, journal reflection, letter.

Showcase: Share a few of the most creative and humorous excuses.

＊ ＊ ＊

Sample Scenarios

- Undone homework
- Late for supper/practice/school
- Telling of a secret
- Lost books/little sister/pet/pencil/money
- Broken ornament/TV/video game/glasses
- Black eye/torn clothes/missing tooth
- Possession of kitten/puppy/new bike/new hat/jacket/shoes
- Lost tech device (smart phone, tablet)/important personal possession (glasses)
- Being caught on restricted Internet site or watching restricted TV show

---

Brainstorm

Subject: Language Arts

Small Groups

Props: One piece of paper per group; a writing tool per student.

Note: Use subject-related words to be reinforced: e.g., *equilateral, Mesopotamia, equation, geography*

152. Break-up

Objective: To break large words into as many smaller words as possible.

- *With your group members, make as many small words as you can from the word I provide.*
- *You can use only the letters in the given word as many times as they appear there. So if the word is "apple," you can use two p's in the words you make. If the word is "pear," then you have only one p to use.*
- *The group with the most words wins.*

＊ ＊ ＊

Sample Words

- multicultural
- extraordinary
- catastrophic
- spaghetti
- pumpernickel
- brainstorming

Brainstorm

Subjects: Any as source of subject; Language Arts

Small Groups

Props: One piece of paper and one writing tool per group

153. Word Expansion

Objective: To generate words and phrases that are related to a given word

- *I will be giving you a general word. In your groups, come up with as many words as possible that are somehow related to that word.*
- *For example, if I give you the word "rain," you might come up with "umbrella," "watering the plants," or "dreary."*
- *You have to be able to justify the words you choose, so if you choose a word like "dreary" you should know how that relates to "rain": i.e., it relates in that usually rainy days are dreary.*
- *Many words can work as long as you know why you have chosen them.*
- *Pick a recorder who will write down your group's choices*
- *This is a competition. The group with the most logical words/phrases wins.*
- Provide a word. Cue to begin. Decide on the winning group at the end.

*   *   *

Sample Words

- sport, team or individual: skating, skiing, hockey
- a natural occurrence or weather-related natural disaster: volcano, storm, drought
- a big news items (but keep it positive): election, opening
- a current school-related situation or event: track-and-field day, parent/teacher interviews

---

Brainstorm

Subject: Any

Small Groups

Props: One piece of paper and one writing tool per student

154. If They Could Talk

Objective: To brainstorm all the things inanimate objects might say, if they could talk.

- *Take out a piece of paper and something to write with.*
- *Your group is going to use your combined imaginations to brainstorm about what inanimate objects might be thinking and saying if they could.*
- *I will give you the name of an inanimate object (something without life), and you will think of all the things that object might say if it were alive. For example, if I say "apple," you might write, "Please don't eat me," or "I want to be in a pie."*
- *You will have 60 seconds to think. Then we'll share a few of your ideas.*

Extended Debrief: Use the brainstormed ideas as story starters or discussion openers.

Showcase: Share a couple of the ideas, then have students keep them for extended debriefing at a later time.

Brainstorm
Subject: Language Arts
Partners

155. First and Last

Objective: To quickly provide a word that begins with the last letter of the word provided by the previous person or partner.

- *For this game, you will need to concentrate on word spellings.*
- *Your job is to think of a word that starts with the last letter of the word your partner says. For example, if I say "father," my partner has to say a word starting with r, such as* right. *Then I have to think of a word that starts with* t, *and so on.*
- *You have to think and speak as quickly as possible.*
- *This is a competition between you and your partner. If either of you can't think of a word in two seconds, if you repeat a word, or if you say "um" or "uh," the other person wins.*
- *I will give you the first word.* Cue to start by giving a word.

Brainstorm
Subject: Any
Partners

156. Over/Under

Objective: To generate items that could go over or under a provided cue item.

- *Decide who's O and who's U. We will switch halfway through.*
- *I will give you an item to discuss.*
- *O stands for* Over, *so Partner O must say something that can go over the item.*
- *U stands for* Under, *so Partner U must say something that can go under the item.*
- *For example, if I say "bed," Partner O could say "quilt," and U could say "shoes."*
- *The trick is to keep thinking of more and more over and under things until I give the Stop cue.*
- *You can be creative and even silly.*
- Allow about one minute on the first word. Then have students switch roles and provide a different word.

*   *   *

Sample Words

- tree
- bush
- clouds
- mushroom
- lake
- rainbow

Brainstorm

Subject: Any as source of sentences; Language Arts

Small Groups

Props: One piece of paper and one writing tool per group; sentences

Prep: Compile a number of sentence starters

Note: The cloze technique encourages students to think critically and analytically about text, and to use written cues to determine meaning while reading.

157. Cloze-it

Objective: To generate creative endings for sentences.

- *In your groups, you will brainstorm to find interesting endings to sentences.*
- *Creativity is the key.*
- *Don't stop at the first ending you come up with. Keep going until you can't think of any more endings or I until give the Stop cue.*
- *Choose a group member to be the recorder. This person will quickly jot down all your clozes.*
- Provide a sentence starter both orally and in written form. Allow two minutes (or more) for groups to brainstorm. The refocuser can end there—the creativity involved is stimulating in itself—or be taken to debriefing.

Debrief: Share and discuss some of the endings, pointing out how the meanings of sentences that start the same all differ according to the endings.

* * *

Sample Sentence Starters

- When the sun is shining…
- It was so terrifying when…
- The nasty creature turned…
- We were very excited because…
- Everything was quiet and then…
- It was a perfect day until…
- I was so happy that I started laughing and then…

Brainstorm

Subject: Language Arts

Small Groups

Props: One piece of paper and one writing tool per group

158. Oxy-challenge

Objective: To generate as many oxymorons as possible in two minutes.

- *We all know what an oxymoron is. It's the putting together of two ideas that seem opposite.*
- *Sometimes oxymorons involve more than two words, like "make haste slowly," but usually they are two words, such as "awfully good" or "almost totally." Discuss quickly why these are oxymorons.*
- *In your groups, think of as many oxymorons as possible until I cue you to stop.*
- *This is a competition. The group with the most oxymorons wins.*
- *Choose one person to be the recorder and write down your choices.*
- Give the Start cue. Stop them when you feel the time is appropriate.

Debrief: Choose a winning group. Invite each group to share their favorite oxymoron.

Extended Debrief: Do an Internet search for ten favorite oxymorons. Assign a writing task that discusses all/some of these.

5

Beyond the Three-Minute Mark

The activities in this section often *stretch* the 3-minute limit, and have, therefore, been separated. Although these activities may take longer to execute—sometimes up to ten minutes or more—they still work well as refocusers or motivators, and anticipatory sets, as long as teachers debrief in such a way as to return students' focus to the interrupted lesson or to turn their attention to the topic to be studied.

These activities involve the whole class in challenging, enjoyable, and intrinsically motivating pursuits. They involve cognition, short-term memory, and all manner of communication, listening, and viewing. Many of them encourage laughter—there is nothing more contagious or powerful than laughter as a teaching tool.

Many of these motivators require props in the form of index cards, written directions, etc. Since coming up with these at the moment a motivator is needed takes away from the spontaneous nature of the refocuser, I suggest having an aide or volunteer—or even an older student—prepare ahead of time. Looking for an activity for a parent helper? This kind of volunteer prep is perfect.

Although the motivators in this chapter are marked as being for small-group or partner work, any of them will work with the whole class.

Frequently an element of competition is involved, together with consistently required cooperation. Often two or more students are It; they may be asked to leave the room for a few moments until the class is ready, then return to engage in a mutually entertaining challenge. Students generally *want* to be It. Once they realize the activity is fun, they are eager to be the "main characters."

- Teachers should remind students of the importance of respect, of *no wrong responses*, and of demonstrating appreciation for individual efforts.
- I find it helpful to supply small rewards, (see page 19) for the student volunteers who take the leading roles in some of these activities.
- Naturally, students should never be forced to be It; however, it is important to encourage students to take turns, especially if the same few are always eager to volunteer.

Beyond the Three-Minute Mark
Subject: Any
Partners as part of Whole Class

Note: This refocuser requires trust, which must be built over time. So if some students are unwilling to be blindfolded, allow them to peek. This activity is not meant to frighten or frustrate, but to be enjoyable.

159. Obstacle Course

Objective: To lead a "blind" partner through an obstacle course of people.

- Begin by dividing the class into two groups. One group (Group O) will be the obstacles, while the other group (Group T) takes the Trust Walk. Halfway through the activity, you can reverse the groups.
- *This game involves trust. You will need to really trust your partner.*
- *Group O, I want you to position yourselves any way you want to, as long as your body presents an obstacle in the room. For example, you might spread your arms and legs into an X, or you might sit down and be a "rock."*
- *Group T, you will have to get past these obstacles from one side of the room to the other. In pairs, decide who's A and who's B.*
- *Partner A, you are the first follower. That means you must shut your eyes during the game, and keep them shut until your partner has led you past the obstacles.*
- *Partner B, you have to carefully lead your partner past the obstacles. You can talk to your partner, guide her or him by the shoulders—whatever. But you must be responsible; don't let your partner get hurt.*
- Allow both groups to experience being both followers and leaders. You might wish to separate this into two activities, rather than have both O and T groups go through the entire experience at once.

Debrief: Quickly discuss how it felt to be leader, follower, and obstacle.

Extended Debrief: Discuss at length various situations in which trust is imperative. This could be extended to a discussion about professions for which trust is involved (e.g., police officers).

Beyond the Three-Minute Mark
Subjects: Language Arts; Math; Science
Whole Class

Note: Students quickly get the idea of responding in a more and more revealing manner, so that the volunteers build up knowledge to come up with guesses. This is a constant work in progress, with learning going on for all.

160. Let's Quiggle

Objective: To guess, by asking pertinent questions, what activity the class has secretly selected.

- *This is a guessing game.*
- *I need two volunteers to leave the room for about 30 seconds. When they return, they will have to guess what activity, such as* eating, *the rest of us have chosen.*
- *The activity will represent an action word, a verb.*
- *The volunteers are It, and will ask Yes/No questions using the word "quiggle" for the activity to be guessed. For example, if we choose* eating *and they ask, "Do you quiggle at home?" we answer, "Yes." If they ask "Are you quiggling all the time?" we answer, "No."*
- *They will ask questions until they think they can guess the secret word. They get three guesses.*
- Discuss briefly, or provide another example (e.g., *breathing*) until students have the idea. Remind them that the secret activity is a verb or action word.
- Send the volunteers out of the room. *Okay, we need to think of a good action word that can end in –ing.*
- Bring volunteers back in and let the fun begin.

- If It students are stuck, prompt them to use leading questions that start with *who, when, where, why, how*. For example:

  Who do you quiggle with most often?
  When/where/why do you quiggle?
  How do you quiggle? (For *eating,* the response can be a vague *"with difficulty"* or as specific as *"by using my mouth and teeth."*)

- Or you can provide more specific clues, such as *"I like to quiggle when I'm hungry."*

Beyond the Three-Minute Mark
Subjects: Health & Wellness; Language Arts; Math; Science
Small Group

Prep: Collect riddles; books and the Internet are good sources

Note: The sample riddles were taken from *Colorful Lateral Thinking Puzzles,* Paul Sloane & Des MacHale, Sterling Publishing.

161. Give Me a Clue

Objective: To figure out the answers to riddles, using leading clues provided by the teacher.

- Begin by getting students into groups as quickly as possible.
- *As a group, your job will be to figure out the answers to some riddles.*
- *I will give you clues.*
- *The first group to find the answer wins (gets a point).*
- Present a riddle.
- Present one clue at a time, allowing about 30 seconds group-talk time before presenting the next clue.
- Continue in this manner.
- If students do not get the answer, provide it fairly quickly so as to maintain the momentum of the game. Use as few or as many riddles as is necessary to refocus or set.
- Any riddles can be used by simply providing a series of consistently more revealing clues.

Debrief: Discuss the importance of looking at all details and thinking in different ways.

Extended Debrief: Challenge students to create their own riddles with clues.

*   *   *

Sample Riddles for Give Me A Clue

1. What is the only day that doesn't end in a *-y*?
   Clues:
   - It is the day we all look forward to.
   - It arrives many times a week.
   - Procrastinators love this day.
   Answer: Tomorrow
2. What is unusual about the number 40?
   Clues:
   - This is not a mathematical property.
   - 40 is different from any other number.
   - It has to do with order.
   - It has a lot to do with spelling.
   - It has a lot to do with the alphabet.
   Answer: Forty is the only number whose letters are in alphabetical order.

Beyond the Three-Minute Mark

Subjects: Language Arts; Math; Science

Whole Class

Props: Small slips of paper

Prep: Write a word on each slip of paper

Note: This refocuser is similar to Give Me A Clue (page 121) in that it involves making guesses based on clues; it differs in that students are not allowed to ask questions. Teacher-provided hints or clues move gradually from general to specific.

162. Specifics, Please

Objective: To guess a word based on effective questioning strategies

- *In this game, you will try to figure out the word I have written on this small slip of paper.*
- *I will give you hints or clues and will keep track of how many you need to solve the problem.*
- *We will play the game a few times. The goal is to use fewer hints than the last time, so you must think about the hints and put them together to make good guesses.*
- Start with general cues. The idea is to use hints that move from general to more and more specific, and to allow several guesses with each hint. The sequence of hints for the word *teacher* might look like this:

  living; human; female; nearby; in the school; in this room; adult

- Keep a tally of the number of hints needed. Of course, the difficulty of the word will affect the number of hints required, but keep the tally nevertheless.
- This is a game—anything goes. Just have fun with it.

Debrief: This is a great discussion-starter about where/when/why/how in life we have to make guesses based on not enough information, and what happens if/when we make incorrect choices as a result.

*   *   *

Sample Words

- animals
- classroom tools or items
- teachers or staff members; by position or by name
- subject-based words that fit with current study; e.g., *element* from Science; *equilateral* from Math

Subjects: Language Arts; Math; Social Studies

Whole Class

Note: Although this activity might seem complicated, students catch on quickly and thoroughly enjoy it.

163. The Rule Rules!

Objective: To figure out what rule or qualifier students are using when they answer Yes/No questions.

- *For this game, volunteers will guess what rule the rest of the class is using when they answer Yes/No questions. The rule could be something like, "Every second person must answer No."*
- *Two student volunteers will leave the room. While outside, they should think of two or three simple questions to which responses will be only Yes or No.*
- *The questions should be ones that you already know the correct answers to. For example, you might ask "Are you sitting down?" You already know everyone is sitting, so when you get a No answer, that gives you a clue.*
- *The volunteers will ask the same question of several students in sequence and, based on their answers, try to figure out the rule.* Model this with the "Are you sitting down?" question. If every second person is answering No, then the first person answers Yes, second answers No, third answers Yes, and so on.
- *Volunteers get three guesses at the rule.*
- *If you think of funny questions, like "Are you a monkey?" some students might have to answer Yes, because they will have to follow the rule.*
- *Volunteers, please leave.* While they are outside, decide on a rule with the class. Rules can be based on sequence (as in the in-text example), physical appearance of students, or actions the students take before answering.
- Initially I let volunteers know which of the three forms of rules—sequence, appearance, or actions—we are using; once the class is familiar with the game, I can omit this information and students will still frequently be successful.
- Call volunteers back and let them begin. If they are stuck, help them by suggesting a question yourself and quickly asking a number of students so that the rule becomes apparent.

*   *   *

Sample Rules Based on Physical Appearance

- All those wearing blue jeans/glasses/sneakers/shorts answer No.
- All those with curly hair answer Yes.
- All those who have on watches answer No.
- All those with books on their desks answer Yes.

Sample Rules Based on Actions

Answer honestly, and do the following as you answer or before you answer:

- Touch your face
- Cough slightly
- Say, "Hmmmm"
- Take a big, deep breath
- Lean forward
- Lift one foot off the floor
- Scratch your head
- Put your hands together
- Bite your lip
- Look up at the ceiling

Beyond the Three-Minute Mark
Subjects: Math; Social Studies
Small Group

Props: Pencil and paper

Prep: Photocopy or print designs on paper; divide each image into thirds with horizontal lines

Note: This is an excellent activity for a very differentiated class in which some students do not speak the language very well.

164. Back Talk

Objective: To copy a design based on tactile impressions put on students' backs.

- Get students into groups, standing in rows, each person facing the back of the person in front. The front person has a pencil and piece of paper. The back person has the image or design.
- *This is a game like the telephone game, in which you pass a whisper. But this time you will pass a picture.*
- *Each illustration is divided into three parts: top, middle, bottom.*
- *The person at the back of the line with the picture must draw the top part of the picture on the back of the person in front of him or her, using only a finger.*
- *Then that person draws on the back of the next person, and so on, until the top part of the drawing reaches the front person.*
- *The front person uses his/her pencil and paper to draw what he or she thinks was drawn on his/her back, then holds up the pencil to show the person at the end of the line that he/she is finished.*
- *As soon as the back person sees the raised pencil, he/she draws the middle part of the illustration on the back of the person in front of him/her, and so on until the entire illustration is reproduced by the person in front.*
- *Remember—no talking. This is not a race; take your time. When everyone's finished we'll see which group is closest to the original drawing.*

Debrief: Discuss the finished pictures.

Showcase: Showcasing the finished illustrations is a natural conclusion, and is often quite humorous.

* * *

Sample Designs

Make sure the outline is clear and the lines are simple and dark. Children's coloring books have excellent, simple illustrations you could use as models. Perfection is unimportant, as the drawing will be greatly distorted anyway.

- Stick person with some identifying characteristic, such as a briefcase, big hat, or funny hair
- Fish with interesting gills or fins
- Tree with various fruits or flowers on it
- Happy face with unusual eyes, hair, hat, earrings
- Simple animal with some unusual characteristic, such as rabbit with bow, donkey with boots
- House made entirely of shapes: i.e., a triangle roof, rectangle door

Beyond the Three-Minute Mark

Subjects: Language Arts; Social Studies

Whole Class

Prep: Choose or write a short story with many details

Note: The story can deliberately be left unfinished (see sample below) so that it can be used for story completion by writing, discussing, or illustrating.

165. Tell It Like It Is

Objective: To repeat a story several times and note the changes in content.

- *For this game, four or five volunteers will wait outside while I tell someone a story.*
- *One at a time, the volunteers will return, listen to the story, then retell it to the next volunteer, until everyone has heard the story.*
- *The last volunteer to hear it must retell it to all of us.*

Debrief: If the story "morphed" a great deal (which it usually does), discuss the reasons for this. If it came out almost the same, discuss the reasons for this.

Extended Debrief: If the story is left unfinished, it provides a great way to begin a writing assignment.

* * *

Sample Story

A boy and his shaggy dog, Bean, were playing catch with an old stick when suddenly the dog darted off into the woods. Naturally, the boy, worried about his dog, followed. The woods were dark and scary; towering trees blocked the sun and thick foliage muffled all sound. The boy stopped. To be sure, he was rather worried about going deeper into the forest, and yet he was also worried about Bean. He called out quietly, "Bean"; then a bit louder, "BEAN." At that very moment he heard a rustling behind him and froze. His imagination ran wild. Was it a monster? An evil sorcerer? A kidnapper? An alien? "B-B-b-b-b-ean," he stammered and then…

Beyond the Three-Minute Mark

Subjects: Any as source of new vocabulary; Language Arts

Whole Class

Props: Word cards

Prep: To make word cards, print unusual words or unfamiliar vocabulary from core subjects on one side of index cards or slips of paper; print pronunciation guides and definitions on the other side.

Note: If you keep index cards readily available and daily add a word or two as they are covered in subjects, it will not take long for a good-sized deck to accumulate.

166. Sense or Nonsense?

Objective: To determine which of several volunteers is providing the real definition for an unusual and unfamiliar word.

- *This is a word-guessing challenge—three volunteers against the rest of the class.*
- *The volunteers will leave the room with a card that has an unusual word on it.*
- *They will decide which among them will provide you with the real meaning; the other two will give you false meanings.*
- *You, as a class, will guess who is telling the truth.*
- *We'll guess by a show of hands after all three volunteers have given their meanings.*
- *If the majority of the class guesses the correct definition, the class wins. If the volunteers manage to confuse you, they win.*
- With younger children, you might want to provide three meanings on the card back: one true meaning and two false ones. Older children enjoy creating the false meanings themselves; they soon discover that creating a false meaning based at least partially on some component of the word serves to confuse the class.

Debrief: Ask students what clues the words could have provided to their actual meanings.

*   *   *

Sample Words

- ULULATE   "you-you-late": to wail or howl loudly
- EFFLUVIUM   "ef-floo-vee-um": an often foul-smelling outflow or vapor
- CASTELLATED   "cas-tell-ate-ed": having turrets or battlements
- ZYMURGY   "zee-mur-gee": technological chemistry of the fermentation process
- VINEGARROON   "vin-i-gar-roon": a large nonvenomous scorpion-like arachnid
- TRUNCATE   "trun-kate": to shorten by cutting off

Beyond the Three-Minute Mark

Subjects: Language Arts; Social Studies

Whole Class

167. It's MY Story!

Objective: To determine which volunteer is the one that a story actually happened to.

- *Three volunteers will leave the room for a few minutes.*
- *While there, they must think of something interesting that actually happened to one of them. When they return each person will say it happened to him or her.* It is helpful to give a quick example here; e.g., "If Tommy had a bad time at the dentist, Sara would say it happened to her, and Don would say it happened to him."
- To the volunteers: *You will need to have enough information about the actual event so that two of you can tell the story convincingly. Your job is to fool the class. If the majority of the class chooses the wrong storyteller, you three are the winners.*
- *The class will be allowed to ask each of you questions. You will answer just as if you were the person in the situation. Naturally, for one of you this will be easy; the other two will have to think quickly and try to answer sensibly.*
- While the volunteers are out, prepare the class by telling them: *Watch for nonverbal cues, such as nervous actions. Ask questions that will give you good information. Ask the same question to more than one volunteer and compare the answers. See if the volunteers trip themselves up in any way.*
- Bring the volunteers back in and allow about five minutes of class questioning; then vote as to which volunteer the class thinks actually had the experience.

Debrief: Ask students what clues the volunteers gave as to whether or not they were telling the truth, and how this information could help them when doing research or collecting data.

Beyond the Three-Minute Mark

Subjects: Language Arts; Science; Social Studies

Whole Class

Props: Profession cards

Prep: To make profession cards, write a profession on each index card or slip of paper

168. The Expert

Objective: To volunteer to become an expert on a skill or profession, and be questioned by peers.

- Ask for volunteers. The number will depend on the amount of time you have. Each volunteer can take from two to five minutes.
- Provide profession cards for random selection. *Please pick a card.*
- *Tell the class the general topic you are an expert in. Are you in the medical field, services, a trade?*
- Allow a few moments for experts to give general hints.
- You can do this part for younger children by giving the class a heads-up about what is to come and helping the "experts" begin to narrow their thinking. For example, if a student picks the *Laboratory assistant* card, you might say, "*This expert is in the helping field. What she does is helpful to others.*" Obviously, the types of vocations will depend on the ages of the students involved.
- Tell the volunteers: *Leave the room; you have two minutes to become experts in whatever is on the index card you selected. When you return, we will question you about your new career. You will answer as if you really are that person. You might want to alter the way you stand, talk, or whatever, to seem more like that expert.*
- While the volunteers are out of the room, say to the class: *Let's think of how we can ask good questions of them. What sorts of questions might we ask? This is not a guessing game, just a form of entertainment.* Allow students to suggest a few questions. These will flow easily once the interview has begun.
- Bring volunteers back. Be prepared to help with the interview if students get bogged down.

Debrief: After each expert, quickly provide positives about the student's ability to represent.

Extended Debrief: Challenge students to think of unusual experts. Record these for future games. Invite students to write about an expert of their choice.

*   *   *

Sample Experts for Grade 5 and Up

- Shoemaker for Aladdin
- Toothpick tester
- Artificial-smoke maker for a rock band
- Guitar-string maker
- Felt-pen filler
- Fish gutter
- Chocolate-bar taster
- Lemon squeezer
- Babysitter
- Stargazer
- Hospital bed-maker
- Space-ship janitor

Sample Experts for Younger Students

- Veterinarian
- Dentist
- Firefighter
- Doctor
- Teacher
- Dog walker
- Police officer
- Courier delivery person

Beyond the Three-Minute Mark

Subjects: Language Arts; Science; Social Studies

Whole Class

Note: If students have difficulty thinking quickly of at-the-desk actions, help them by offering some from the list below.

169. And the Action Is…

Objective: To guess the adverbs that are controlling actions performed by peers.

- *This is a game that involves good questioning techniques.*
- *Two volunteers at a time will leave the room. While outside, they will think of some actions to request of the rest of the class. In other words, they will decide on things they will ask the rest of us to do right at our desks. For example, they might ask someone to stand up or someone else to stretch.*
- *The actions must be the kind that can be easily done.*
- *But here's the catch. When the person does the action, he or she will do it according to the describer—the adverb—we have chosen in the classroom. For example, if we have chosen the adverb* slowly, *then when I am asked to stand up, I do it very slowly. But I don't say anything about what I am doing.*
- *It's the volunteers' job to figure out the adverb* slowly *by the way I am reacting.*
- *The volunteers can ask up to five people to do actions before they have to guess. Then they have three guesses.*
- *If the volunteers don't guess the action by that time, the game is over!*

Debrief: Discuss what is known about use of adverbs; e.g., most (probably all those chosen) end in *–ly*.

Extended Debrief: Use adverbs in a writing task.

*   *   *

Sample Actions

- clap
- stand
- reach
- yawn
- bend

- touch toes
- laugh
- cry
- shake hand with neighbor
- stand and turn around

- march in place while sitting/standing
- play peek-a-boo with hands over eyes
- tap toes

Beyond the Three-Minute Mark

Subjects: Language Arts; Science; Social Studies

Whole Class

Note: The English language has many short phrases that mean *good-bye*. With younger students, you might want to stick with these other ways of saying good-bye, and not deal with the more abstract concept of finishing off.

70. Forever After

Objective: To generate phrases that suggest something is finished

- *Think of how we say good-bye. There are many different ways.* Invite students to share a few.
- *Now think of words that suggest an ending, a finishing, a releasing, or a closing of a situation, thing, or idea. For example, some people say "I wash my hands of this"; it means that they want nothing more to do with it.*
- *In your groups, brainstorm for any words/phrases that suggest this sort of finishing off. You can use common "good-bye" terms too, but try to be creative.*

Debrief: Discuss the difficulty involved in saying good-bye or stopping/ending anything abruptly.

Extended Debrief: Do an Internet search for ways to say good-bye in other languages. Encourage creativity with older students. Have them make up their own new ways to indicate something is over.

* * *

Sample Phrases to Indicate Finishing

- Tie a knot/bow in it
- Slam the door on it
- Wrap/zip/tie/wind it up
- Wipe/wash your hands of it
- Shred/discard/burn it, throw it away
- Put a lock on it
- Lock it and throw away the key
- Say, "That's a wrap"
- Say, "May the force be with you"
- That's it!
- Over and out
- Sign off
- That's a big 10-4
- Send/delete/recycle/close/save

Common English Ways to Say "Good-bye"

- "Farewell."
- "See you."
- "Later."
- "So long."
- "All right, then."
- "Peace." or "Peace off."
- "Good day."
- "Cheers."
- "Catch you later."
- "Have a good one."
- "Take care."
- "Be well."

Beyond the Three-Minute Mark
Subject: Language Arts
Partners

Props: One piece of paper and one writing tool per partnership; ScraPPle Alphabet

Prep: Post a ScraPPle Alphabet of letters and their point values

Notes:
- If you want to increase the difficulty and connect this motivator directly to subject content, have students make words related to a specific theme. If you do this, have them choose six or more letters.
- If you use this motivator more than once, it's a good idea to change the letter values. Students are experts at remembering which letters have the most value, so mix it up.

171. ScraPPle

Objective: To make words that earn points.

- *This game is like Scrabble, but it's called ScraPPle because it's not quite the same.*
- *With your partner, choose five letters of the alphabet, but no vowels. Write them on the top of your page.* You might decide to have students use more/fewer letters, depending on student ages/abilities.
- *Look at my ScraPPle Alphabet and write under each letter how much that letter is worth. For example, if you chose S, you'll see an S is worth one point, so you write 1 under your S.*
- Show the ScraPPle Alphabet on an overhead, chart paper, or interactive whiteboard. Allow students time to identify the letter values.
- *You notice there are no vowels on the alphabet. Vowels are free—you can use as many as you want wherever you want, but you don't gain points for them.*
- *Now your job is to create as many real words as you can with your chosen letters and any vowels you need. You can use the letters as many times as you want, but you can use* only *the letters you already selected.*
- *When I cue you to stop, you will count up all the points you have earned.*

* * *

Sample ScraPPle Alphabet

B = 2	J = 6	Q = 7	X = 7
C = 2	K = 5	R = 3	Y = 4
D = 1	L = 2	S = 1	Z = 8
F = 4	M = 2	T = 1	
G = 4	N = 2	V = 5	
H = 3	P = 3	W = 5	

Subjects: Any as source of theme; Language Arts

Small Groups

Props: Paper and writing tools

Notes: Poetry provides a powerful outlet for feelings. Writing it is cathartic and actually helps reduce negative emotions.

172. Passion Poem

Objective: To follow a specific format and write a passionate poem.

- The poems in this activity are based on cinquain poetry, but have been renamed to indicate a passionate response to a troublesome situation. Use this refocuser when the class is concerned, upset, or annoyed about something; e.g., homework frustration, wet weather preventing an outdoor pursuit. The class's negative emotions become the topics for the passion poems.
- *Right now we are all feeling concerned/upset/ annoyed because _____.*
- *So in groups you get to express passionately how you are feeling.*
- *Work together to come up with a poem describes how you feel at this moment.*
- *Follow this outline:*

    Line 1: The topic, your strong emotion. Write it as a noun
    Line 2: Two describing words, or adjectives, that further explain that emotion.
    Line 3: Three action words, or verbs, that have to do with the emotion. These might tell what you feel like doing, or what you would like to be doing.
    Line 4: Four words that tell what you wish was different, what change you would like to see
    Line 5: One word that sums it all up

- Show or write a sample poem.
- You might wish to discuss briefly what negative emotions are obvious in the class at that time. This will help students get started.
- Allow about five or six minutes, no more. The poems should be spontaneous.
- Share the poems.

Debrief: Discuss how writing the poems was helpful, or not.

* * *

Sample Passion Poem

Anger
Quick, loud
Shaking, clenching, frowning
Homework should be less
Overwhelmed

Subjects: Language Arts; Social Studies

Whole Class working in Small Groups

Props: Action Cards (optional)

Prep: Prepare Action Cards by writing an action scenario on each index card or slip of paper.

Notes:

- Instead of using Action Cards, you could write actions on the board for the last students in their lines to see. Then quickly erase these cues. This makes the motivator a bit more spontaneous, as long as you can quickly come up with a sequence of actions.
- Remind students that, although the game is called Action *Telephone*, no conversation is allowed.

173. Action Telephone

Objective: To pass a message conveyed only through actions, and watch how it changes.

- *For this game, your group will stand in a line, all facing the same direction.* Be sure to provide a space for each group.
- *The person at the end of the line will be given an Action Card.*
- *He or she will tap the person in front of him/her on the shoulder. That person will turn around and watch as the person acts out whatever is on the card. At this point, only two people will be involved—the actor and the watcher.*
- *The second-last person (the watcher) will then tap the person in front of him or her and repeat acting out the action, and so on until the front person has received the message.*
- *The person at the front of the line remembers the action sequence until it is time to share it with the rest of us.*
- *No talking in this game. It's all done by actions.*
- *When your group is finished, sit down on the floor and wait for directions.*
- *This is not a speed challenge. It is a game of communication.*
- When all groups are sitting, call on the front student in each line to act out the sequence.

Debrief: Discuss how the original message changed, or not.

*   *   *

Sample Actions

- Changing a tire
- Changing a baby's diaper
- Making a cake/pizza/any meal
- Giving someone a shave and a haircut
- Bathing a big shaggy dog
- Eating ice cream/spaghetti/hot soup
- Picking up garbage in a park
- Doing dishes
- Looking for lost keys/homework/ books
- Digging up worms for fishing
- Using super glue that sticks to the wrong things

Subjects: Art; Language Arts; Science

Partners

Props: Paper and writing/coloring tools

Note: This refocuser can start during a lesson as a 3-Minute Motivator and then become part of an Art class, or even a Language Arts writing class. The initial creativity can be the refocuser; the rest of the work can be done later.

174. A-One Superhero

Objective: To create a superhero.

- *Have you noticed how many movies, cartoons, and TV shows are about superheroes?*
- *With your partner, you are going to create the best A-one superhero. Your superhero can be male, female, animal, human…whatever you want.*
- *First decide what his/her special power(s) will be, then create the hero to fit those powers.*
- *Then think of a name, a costume, and an attitude.*
- *If you have time, think of a particular phrase or expression—even a jingle—that your superhero might use all the time.*
- *Have fun with this.*

Beyond the Three-Minute Mark
Subject: Language Arts
Small Groups

Props: Two or three rolls of toilet paper

175. Toilet Tales

Objective: To tell a tale as a group.

- Give each group of four or five a roll of toilet paper.
- Have students pass around the roll. Each student tears off as many squares as he/she wants. At this point they do not know what the squares are for.
- Collect the rolls (to prevent taking more squares as the tales progress) and tell students: *Now you are going to work together to tell a story.*
- *Each person can say only as many words as he/she has squares of paper. In other words, I have two squares, so I get to add two words each time the tale comes to me.*
- *You can't discuss what the story is about. You just have to let it grow on its own. But it has to make some sense.*
- *Keep going around the circle, adding your words according to how many squares you have. If you come to a natural end of a sentence, say "period," then begin a new sentence.*
- Choose one person in each group to start and allow students to begin after you give the opening *"Once upon a time there was a..."*
- The tale can move around the circle several times, but each student always adds only as many words as tissue squares they hold.
- Allow a few minutes then cue for silence. Invite students to share as much of their stories as they can remember.

Beyond the Three-Minute Mark
Subjects: Language Arts; Science
Partners

Props: One slip of paper per student

Prep: Fortunes written on index cards (optional)

Notes: An alternative is to have a series of fun fortunes already written on index cards (see below). Just hand them out randomly and enjoy.

176. Fortuneteller

Objective: To write and share fortunes like the ones in fortune cookies.

- *With your partner, you will be a fortuneteller today.*
- *When I give the Start cue, write a fortune on your slip of paper. They should be like the fortunes that come in fortune cookies.*
- Discuss this if necessary, pointing out that fortunes are always rather vague and non-specific. You might consider writing one together first.
- Give the Start cue. Collect finished fortunes in a container.
- Have students randomly pick fortunes and read them aloud. Enjoy the laughter and silly fun—remember, there is a place for silly in every classroom.

* * *

Sample Fortunes

For very young students, allow very simple fortunes, such as "Good luck," and "Have fun today." Fortunes for older students can be longer and more detailed:

- All your hard work will pay off soon.
- Your smile brightens up the day.
- You will get a big surprise tomorrow.
- Congratulations! You are on your way.
- Go with the flow.
- Tomorrow looks bright for you.
- You have a secret admirer.

Beyond the Three-Minute Mark
Subjects: Art; Language Arts
Partners

Props: Paper and writing/coloring tools; flash cards

Prep: Prepare flash cards with the names of people students will recognize

177. Beautiful People

Objective: To draw a person from auditory descriptions only.

- *Decide who's A and who's B.*
- *Partner A, you are the speaker. Partner B, you are the illustrator. You'll switch later.*
- *I am going to hold up a flash card with the name of someone we all know on it.*
- *Partner A, you must get B to draw that person by giving verbal clues only. You cannot use names or positions. For instance, you can't say "Teacher in this room" or "Mayor of this city."*
- *You can say things like "Tall, dark-haired, female."*
- If the "person" on the flash card is a cartoon character, speakers are allowed to say that the person is a cartoon.
- *I'll be walking around to see that no specific clues are given. This is supposed to be fun and funny, so you want your illustrator to have to use some imagination.*
- *Illustrators, if you figure out who your speaker is talking about, don't say a word, just make your illustration as much like that person as you can.*
- Have illustrators close their eyes. Hold up a flash card just long enough for the speakers to see.
- Allow about five minutes per illustration. Some students might actually guess the person; that's okay. Many will not, and the end results can be hilarious.

Debrief: This activity offers insight into how difficult it is to describe using only auditory cues. A healthy discussion can follow.

* * *

Sample Flash Card Names

- staff in the school
- currently studied character from history
- local politician, policeman, storekeeper
- music or movie star
- cartoon character

Beyond the Three-Minute Mark

Subject: Language Arts

Individual

Props: Paper and writing/coloring tools

178. My Favorite Letter

Objective: To write/illustrate/demonstrate why a particular letter is a favorite.

- *Who has ever watched Sesame Street? Do you remember how that show often focuses on a specific letter? It is called the letter of the day.*
- *Now you get to choose your favorite letter. It can be any letter—not necessarily the first letter of you name, although it might be that.*
- *You have (state the amount of time you have available) to cover your page with anything to do with that letter.*
- *You can print, write, draw, color. Do anything you want to show why you have chosen that letter to be your favorite letter right now.*
- Cue to start. If students are stuck, the following prompts might help:

  - *Write the letter in lower and upper case, in all different sizes, shapes, colors.*
  - *Write words that begin with that letter; draw items that begin with that letter.*
  - *Give the letter a personality: a face, legs, arms, etc.*
  - *Write phrases that explain why you chose that letter.*

Showcase: Showcase by displaying all the finished products.

Beyond the Three-Minute Mark

Subject: Language Arts

Individual

Props: One piece of paper and one writing tool per student

Note: This activity is a great getting-to-know-you game at the beginning of the year, but also works beautifully as a refocuser, as it gives students a break from intense solitary work and allows them to think of others for a few minutes.

179. I Know You!

Objective: To interview peers, then report back to the class.

- *First divide your page into quarters. Then write the numbers 1, 2, 3 vertically at the left side of each quadrant.*
- *When I give the Start cue, move around the room and interview four other students by asking each of them two questions. Ask these two questions: What is your favorite _____. Choose food/TV show/music star/ song/etc. And what is your current pet peeve?*
- *Beside the number 1 in the first quadrant you will write the first person's name*
- *Beside the numbers 2 and 3 you will write the responses to the questions.*
- *Fill in the other quadrants with three other people you interview.*
- *There will be some confusion if everyone is trying to interview everyone else, so you'll have to figure out a system as you go. Quickly check to see who is free at any moment and go to that person.*
- *You will have only six minutes to interview four people, so you'll have to work quickly. You might not get all four of your quadrants filled, and that's okay.*
- *When I cue you to stop, return to your desks for the next part of this activity.*
- Allow no more than six minutes. By then all students will have some interviews completed.
- *Now I will call out a name, and if you have information about that person, you can call it out. For example, if I call "Alan," and Becky interviewed Alan, she could call out "likes pizza." If several people have interviewed Alan, we'll take turns sharing what we know about him.*

Note: Although this seems like a quick motivator, it can lead to some lengthy discussions when groups cannot agree on which modern appliance should go.

180. I Could Live Without It

Objective: To come to a group decision about which modern appliance we could manage best without.

- *Today we have so many modern appliances that work we do at home is very different from what it was like in settler days.*
- *Let's brainstorm for all the appliances in our homes.* Do this as a group for a few moments so students begin to realize just how many appliances we have: e.g., refrigerators, stoves, microwave ovens, electric kettles, coffee makers, dishwashers, blenders, food processors, etc.
- *Your job, as a group, is to decide which appliance we could do without. If one of them had to go, which one should it be, and why?*
- *You will have five minutes to discuss this. Remember to give a reason for your decision.*
- *Choose a speaker who will share your decision with the rest of us.*

Debrief: This refocuser lends itself to a writing task about then and now, or about our overdependence on objects.

Props: One piece of paper and one writing tool per group

181. Unusual Uses

Objective: To create unusual uses for commonplace objects

- *You have an interesting challenge. In your groups, brainstorm as many uses as you can for the objects I provide.*
- *You need to be very creative. For example, for these scissors, you might say they could be used for sharpening pencils, making clicking sounds in time to music, drawing circles like a compass.*
- *I will give you ____ objects.* Choose two to four, depending on how much time you want to spend on this. Allow at least five minutes per object.
- *Choose one person in your group to record your suggestions.*
- *We will share as soon as the thinking time is up (after we finish Math).*
- Cue to start.
- When time is up, you can debrief, showcase, or put the papers away for future use.

* * *

Sample Objects

- Classroom tools: stapler, scissors, writing tools, paper clips, ruler, etc.
- Keys, jewelry, watches, chains
- Digital devices: cell phones, smart phones, notebooks, MP3 players, tablets, computers, the interactive whiteboard, the projector, etc.
- Kitchen utensils: forks, knives, spoons, plates, pots, coffee pots, blenders, indoor griddles, etc.

Beyond the Three-Minute Mark
Subject: Any
Whole Class

Props: Paper and writing tools for each student

Note: This refocuser can be used only one time, as kids quickly catch on to the trick. However, it is very effective and has considerable learning potential.

182. The Unfair Test

Objective: To appreciate the humor in an unfair test.

- *Take out a pencil and piece of paper for a pop quiz.* Accept the groans and complaints and keep a straight face.
- *Write the numbers 1 to 3.* You can use as many unfair questions as you like; usually three is enough.
- Ask all the questions. Have students exchange papers to "mark."
- *For each question on this test, there is only one correct answer.* Provide the obscure answers that are the only acceptable responses (see below).

Debrief: Discuss situations in life that seem unfair, and what we can do to deal with them in the best way possible. Also discuss the terms *right and wrong*, *trick question*, and *point of view*.

*   *   *

Sample Questions and Acceptable Answers

- What is H2O ?   *A home for a fish*
- What is this? (hold up a pencil)   *A back scratcher*
- What are these? (hold up keys)   *A source of amusement for a little child*
- How do you spell this? (hold up an item)   *T-H-I-S*
- How do you spell this? (hold up a stapler)   *C-L-O-S-E-R*
- What is this? (hold up a ruler)   *A band director's wand*
- What is this? (any coin)   *Something I don't have enough of*

Beyond the Three-Minute Mark
Subjects: Language Arts; Social Studies
Small Groups

Note: This motivator allows students a chance to be playful about themselves and to think critically about peers.

183. Two Truths and a Lie

Objective: To try to distinguish truths from lies.

- *For this game each of you must think of three statements about yourself.*
- *Two of these statements will be true. The third will be a lie.*
- *They will be short sentences. When you tell them to your group, you will, of course, mix up the order of presentation. For example, you might give a truth, then the lie, then another truth.*
- *Let's try it. I might say "I am a good skater." "I love asparagus." "I have been teaching school for ten years."*
- *Now you have to guess which one is the lie.* Allow guessing.
- *I will give you 60 seconds to think of your three statements, then you will share with your group and do the guessing.*
- Cue to think. Then cue to start.

Extended Debrief: This is an excellent anticipatory set for a discussion/lesson about lying vs telling the truth. You can generate a list of reasons for telling the truth: *If you tell the truth…*

- *you don't have to remember anything.*
- *you feel better.*
- *people will more likely trust you in the future.*
- *you are showing integrity and honesty.*

184. Twinkle Twinkle

Objective: To rewrite a popular nursery rhyme

- *We all know "Twinkle, Twinkle, Little Star." Recite as a rhyme or sing:*

  Twinkle, twinkle, little star.
  How I wonder what you are,
  Up above the world so high
  Like a diamond in the sky.
  Twinkle, twinkle, little star.
  How I wonder what you are.

- *When I give the start cue, in your groups/partnerships, you will change the lyrics to that little rhyme.*
- *You can make them as silly, funny, or serious as you want.*
- *Be prepared to sing/say them to the class.*
- Give an example. You can use the one from Lewis Carroll's *Alice's Adventures in Wonderland*, show one of the samples below, or make up one of your own. If your students can handle it in a positive manner, you can suggest they use themselves as their topic.

  *   *   *

Sample Verses

  Twinkle, twinkle, little pot.
  I hear you bubbling quite a lot.
  What foodstuff do you gently simmer?
  I just can't wait until it's dinner.
  …
  Purring, purring, little cat.
  You're all curled up and kind of fat
  Sitting on that chair you own
  Like a queen upon her throne.
  …

Props: One piece of paper and one writing tool per group/partnership

Note: This is an amazing motivator to use as an anticipatory set for lessons on organization or breaking down tasks—areas we all need reminding of and practice in.

185. Nibbles

Objective: To break down tasks into small components.

- *I know you've all had the experience of having to do something that seemed too huge or too scary to ever get done.*
- *In this game we are going to take nibbles, or tiny bites, out of a task.*
- *I will give you an imaginary task. In your groups, try to break it into the smallest bits possible.*
- *You might want to work backward, starting with the finished task and breaking it apart right back to where it began. Or you can simply begin by thinking of how you might start.*
- *In either case, jot down the nibbles in the order they would be taken.*
- *Since these are imaginary tasks, there is no real right or wrong way to accomplish them, but remember to move toward the end in tiny steps or little nibbles.*
- *Select a recorder to jot down the steps as you figure them out together.*

* * *

Sample Tasks

- Make yourselves into a group of superheroes
- Make a spaghetti dinner for a group of 100 friends
- Create a rock band that will perform tonight at _____
- Invent the cure for loneliness/boredom/fear/jealousy
- Design the perfect desk/skateboard/bike/skis/skates
- Take a dog to the Westminster Dog Show
- Design the perfect teacher/sibling/parent/friend

Props: Four small balloons (two each of two colors), two handfuls rice, a pair scissors per partnership

Prep: Collect the materials (balloons, rice); make a sample ball (optional)

Note: The finished products can be collected and kept for tasks for which beanbags would otherwise be used. They can also serve as gifts; e.g., stress balls for adults, toys for younger children.

186. Rockin' Rice Balls

Objective: To make two rice balls per partnership (one per student)

- *You will work with a partner, so that you can help each other.*
- *You will each end up with your own ball.*
- *I will talk you through the steps and we will do them together.*
- *Fill one balloon with a fistful of rice and tie it.*
- *Stretch the other balloon over the first one, being sure to cover the tied end completely*
- *Tie the second one as close as you can to the inner balloon.*
- *Use scissors to cut the tied part as close as possible to the balloon.*
- *Now carefully snip small pieces out of just the outer balloon.* Demonstrate. Students will probably cut through to the inner balloon or cut the holes too large, so have extra balloons on hand. *You will end up with spots of the color of the inside balloon.*
- *Shape the balloon by gently rolling it between your hands until it has a nice spherical shape.*

6

Today and Tomorrow

Some activities in Today and Tomorrow follow the established format for 3-Minute Motivators; others have a more personal in- or out-of-class approach.

In this chapter, new to this edition of *3-Minute Motivators*, consideration is given to the world of today's technology, in which all our students are immersed; also explored is the timely issue of dealing with the stress or anxiety associated with kids' overfilled agendas, both in and out of school. The new challenges and tensions students face today have impact on how children manage learning and living, as students and adults. In giving our students (and ourselves) quick and easy techniques for coping, we are doing everyone a great favor.

Tech Too

Today's students have been raised in a digital environment with computers in their hip pockets, so to speak. They are very familiar with all things technological, so it makes sense to have refocusers that work within this seemingly dominant aspect of their lives. Like all other refocusers in this book, the Motivators in this chapter are quick and easy activities that excite and stimulate students, and provide brief interludes from whatever lessons are being taught.

Tech Too activities all focus to some degree on the digital environment. They are directly related to awareness, understanding, and appreciation of technology in the classroom.

- The activities marked Digital Fingertips require computers with Internet access, making them great refocusers for use *during* a computer-based class. Even with the natural motivation attached to computer-based lessons, students can become restless, distracted, or off-task. All you need to do is cue for attention and have students save what they are working on and close the page. Then they will be ready for the refocuser. It's true that these motivators can take more than three minutes, but if you adhere to time suggestions strictly, they can fit that time allotment.
- The refocusers marked Digital Desks are technology-related, but can be carried out right at students' desks. This makes them easy to incorporate into any lesson, using students' interest in and understanding of technology to help them come back to the lesson with new enthusiasm. All except one are done with partners, so communication skills as well as cognition and memory are reinforced.
- All activities in this section challenge students' understanding of the application of technology and invite them to recall, relate, and even reinvent what they know.

Where activities are marked as *Individual*, please remember that it is simply a suggested guideline.

- Many of these 3-Minute Motivators are individual pursuits, but they can be adapted to address socialization simply by having students work with partners or in small groups

Digital Fingertips

Subject: Any as source of facts; Research

Individual

Prep: Collect true/false facts

Note: This is a wonderful refocuser that also can help students obtain new knowledge or reinforce what is already known, as well as providing practice in research skills.

187. Fact or Fiction

Objective: To do a digital search to determine fact from fiction.

- *We are going to take a few minutes for a change of focus right now.*
- *Stop what you are doing. Close and save your work.*
- *Now listen carefully to the statement I read. You have 60 seconds to try to find out if it is true or not true; that is, whether it is fact or fiction.*
- *You can use your computers to search.*
- Cue to start and to stop, even if not all students have found the answer.

* * *

Sample True/False Facts

- A stranger who stopped to change a tire on a disabled limo was rewarded for his efforts when the vehicle's passenger, Donald Trump, paid off his mortgage. (False)
- A police officer promised a waitress half his earnings if he won the lottery. He won. He gave her half. (True)
- Breaking a mirror brings seven years of bad luck. (Unverifiable)
- Rain that falls during a sun shower brings good luck. (Unverifiable)
- Creating a phony entry in your address book will stop viruses from mailing themselves out from your computer. (False)
- The Stanley Cup was once left in a snowbank. (True)
- Disneyland used to deny admission to long-haired male guests. (True)

Sample Content-Area True/False Facts

- The Great Wall of China is the only human-made object visible from the moon. (False)
- A lightbulb manufactured in 1901 burns brightly to this day. (True)
- A convex (outward) quadrilateral with one pair of parallel sides is known as a trapezoid in the US and a trapezium in other parts of the world. In both instances it comes from a Greek word meaning "little table." (True)
- The sun supplies all energy needed for life. (False: certain microscopic organisms don't get their energy from the sun, but from inorganic sources.)

Subject: Any as source of facts; Research

Partners

Prep: Compile a list of subject ideas

188. Then & Now

Objective: To do a digital search to discover the roots of a modern tool or appliance.

- *I think we can all agree that we live in an ever-changing environment, with new gadgets and appliances and tools appearing daily.*
- *For this game you are to work together to figure out what we used to have or use before an item we have today. We'll call the current item the* today-tool.
- *We will call what came before the current item* past-tools. *For example, if the today-tool is a flat iron for hair, the past-tool might have been _____.* Allow some responses; e.g., clothes iron, ironing board.
- *Use your computers to research for possible past-tools.*
- *There might be more than one past-tool for the today-tool, so keep searching until I cue you to stop.*

* * *

Sample Today-Tools

- computers
- tablets
- smart phones
- iPods
- iPads
- notebook computers
- e-mail
- social networks: Facebook, Instagram, Twitter, etc.

- e-reader
- ear buds
- flash drive
- podcast
- digital photo story
- blog
- cyberbullying

Digital Fingertips

Subject: Any as source of facts; Research

Small Groups

Note: For sample technologies, see samples for Then & Now above.

189. The Good, The Bad, and the Really Awful

Objective: To express subjective opinions about technology.

- *Have you heard someone say that technology today is bad, harmful, causing more problems than it's worth?* Allow a few responses.
- *In this game, you get to make a group decision about specific forms of technology.*
- *I will name a technology. You will decide if it's bad, good, or really really awful. You might even decide that it's a bit of both bad and good.*
- *The catch is that the group must come to one decision, and you have only a few minutes to convince each other.*
- Name a technological device or technologically based behavior.

* * *

Sample Behaviors

- online/video game playing
- online chat/dating/sharing of personal information
- use of e-mail/social networks
- online banking/shopping/business
- unlimited exposure to web pages/specialty sites/adult-only sites

Digital Fingertips

Subject: Any as source of words; Research

Partners

Props: Word-search software

Notes:
- This is a great way to reinforce and review content vocabulary. Completed projects can be printed and used later in class.
- This 3-Minute Motivator can be returned to repeatedly for brief intervals as several refocusers.

190. Tech Search

Objective: To do a word search based on technological (or subject content) words

- *With your partner, you are going to do a word search using as many technology/science/math words as you can think of.* You can have them search generally for subject words, or more specifically for content-area words.
- *First you will have to use your computers to find a good program for making word searches.*
- *I will allow you only three minutes, so you will have to work quickly.* The amount of time can be adjusted according to the situation.
- *When I cue you to stop, save your work and we will return to it later.*

Digital Fingertips

Subject: Any as source of facts; Research

Small Groups

Prep: Prepare a list of devices/ technologies

Note: Students love this activity. If they can't find an object's history, allow some creativity and imagination on their parts and have them make it up.

191. Going Back

Objective: To think backward from a current technology to work through its history.

- *For this game, each group will work on one device or technology.*
- *I will choose a device or technology for you.*
- *Your job will be to think backward from that item, and try to get as far back into history as possible. For example, if the item is a smart phone, you might first go back to a cell phone, then to a cordless land line, then…* Allow a few responses.
- *You can use your computers to search back. You might have to get creative.*
- *Have one group member record all the steps back.*
- *Go as far back as you can in the time allotted.*

* * *

Sample Technologies

- interactive whiteboards
- e-readers
- e-mail
- microwave ovens
- indoor grills
- home theatres
- talking vehicles
- self-parking vehicles
- DVD burners
- robot for surgery
- voice answering systems
- tablets
- tappable credit cards and card readers
- digital gas pumps
- computer servers
- search engines

Digital Fingertips

Subject: Any as source of words; Research

Partners

Props: Online crossword program

Note: Like Tech Search, this 3-Minute Motivator can be broken down into small bursts of work and returned to on several occasions.

192. Tech Cross

Objective: To create a crossword puzzle using only tech (or subject-content) words.

- *With your partner, you will make a fun crossword puzzle, but you can use only words that are related in some way to technology/science/math. You can have them use general subject words, or more specific content-area words.*
- *First you must find a crossword-puzzle maker online.*
- *Collect a list of words.*
- *Remember that for every word, you will need a definition. That's how users of the crossword puzzle will figure out the words. So have succinct, short, accurate definitions of your words as clues.*
- *Use the crossword maker to make your words into a puzzle. This refocuser can be done without the crossword program; have students link the words together as if they were going to place them in a crossword.*

Digital Fingertips

Subject: Any as source of facts; Research

Partners

Prep: Compile a list of unusual words. There are many Internet sites for weird and wonderful words. Have a volunteer or older student research a list for you.

Note: This is usually a very quick activity with hilarious results. You can give a different word to each partnership, so that the results are more entertaining when shared.

193. Unusual & Unique

Objective: To do a digital search to identify unusual or unique words.

- *With your partner, you are going to search the Internet for clues about words provided by me.*
- *The words might be for things, or people, or situations. But they are all unusual or unique.*
- *You must jot down any information you find, and also indicate what is unusual or unique about the word.*
- *The catch is that you can use only ten to fifteen words for each word—no lengthy definitions. You have to keep it short and concise.*
- Give one word at a time, allowing only a few minutes for researching.
- You can take this a step further by inviting students to find unusual or unique items/people/situations and to report back on these.

*   *   *

Sample Words

- jackalope
- knucker
- haberdasher
- interrobang
- rannygazzo
- rumbledethumps

Digital Fingertips

Subject: Research

Partners

Note: This refocuser is great fun for students, and can lead to innovative in-class exploits using the latest technology.

194. I Web 2.0 Too

Objective: To become familiar with Web 2.0 tools and choose one to try in class.

- *On the Internet you can find great sites with programs called Web 2.0 tools.*
- Google "Web 2.0 tools" for sites that list and give links to sites of Web 2.0 tools. Choose one that looks inviting. Digital tools are usually divided into Presentation, Video, Mobile, and Community, so it's best to limit students to one of these categories each time you use this refocuser.
- *You and you partner are going to explore and quickly select a tool you'd like to see us use in class.*
- *You have to skim quickly through a lot of possibilities and then check out the individual sites to find a tool that seems interesting.*
- *Jot down the name of the tool you have chosen, and a few words explaining it.*

Debrief: Have students present their findings.

Extended Debrief: Use students' findings for in-class pursuits.

Digital Desks

Subject: Technology

Partners

Notes:
- This is similar to Word Tennis on page 112, but differs in that only technology-related words are allowed.
- There are many Internet sites that provide extensive technology vocabulary. However, for this refocuser, only words the students have in their minds can be used.

195. Tech Tennis

Objective: To verbally toss technology-related terms back and forth without repetition

- *Sit facing your partner.*
- *Decide who's A and who's B.*
- *When I give the Start cue, start saying words back and forth quickly, without pausing for more than three seconds, and without saying "um" or "er" or hesitating in any other way.*
- *The words must all be related in some way to technology.*
- *Partner B will start. As soon as B says a word, A must say another word, and so on.*
- *If one partner cannot think of any more words, the other wins.*
- *If a word is said that is not a technology word, the other partner wins.*
- *This is for fun, so enjoy the word race.*
- Cue to start. Stop when most seem to be stuck.

Digital Desks

Subject: Technology

Partners

Note: The difference between this activity and Tech Tennis on page 144 is that here each word must trigger the next word in some way. The game is less random, and therefore more difficult.

196. Tech-sion

Objective: To quickly say a technology-related word associated with the previous word.

- *Sit facing your partner.*
- *Decide who's A and who's B.*
- *When I give the Start cue, you will start saying words back and forth quickly, without pausing for more than three seconds, and without saying "um" or "er" or hesitating in any other way.*
- *The words must all be related in some way to technology.*
- *Partner B will start. As soon as B says a word, A must say another word and so on.*
- *But here's the catch. This is* word association. *That means each word must in some way be associated with the word before it. Here's a non-technology example: if the word was* dark, *the next word could be* sky *or* night. *Both of those words are associated with* dark. *If the word associated with* dark *is* night, *the next word has to be somehow related to* night, *like* stars.
- *And remember that, for this game, the words must also be related to technology.*
- *Not every word will necessarily be a technology word; it could be a word that is related but not technological in itself. For example, if the first word is* cell phone, *the next word might be* annoying, *then the next might be* digital games *(which you might feel are annoying), and so on.*
- *Try to keep bringing the associations back to technology.*
- Cue to start. Watch for pairs that get too far off-base and help them return to technology words.

Digital Desks

Subject: Technology

Partners

197. Tech Alpha-Talk

Objective: To carry on a conversation about technology, where each person begins with the next word in alphabetical sequence.

- *Sit facing your partner.*
- *Decide who's A and who's B.*
- *You are going to carry on a conversation about anything techie: computers, games, TV—anything modern and tech-based*
- *But the catch is that, when each person starts to speak, the first word said must start with the next letter of the alphabet. For example, Partner A must start the talk with a word that starts with A: he or she might say, "A computer is a useful tool." Then B will respond, but the first word he/she says must start with B: "But sometimes they break down." Then A might say, "Can you fix your own computer?"*
- *Keep going until you reach the end of the alphabet.*

Digital Desks

Subject: Technology

Partners

Props: Paper and writing tools

Note: This refocuser can be stopped after the brainstorming portion; actually creating the app can be moved to an Art class.

198. Need-an-App

Objective: To design a useful new app.

- *There are so many apps available to us today. What are some of your favorites?* Allow just a few responses.
- *What if you could design a new app? What would it be for? What would it look like?*
- *Your job, with your partner, is to think of an exciting new app that you think will be useful, and then actually design its appearance.*
- *First you need to brainstorm apps that don't already exist.*
- *Then draw, color, etc. to make that app as appealing as possible.*

Digital Desks

Subject: Technology

Partners

Props: Paper and writing tools

Note: Many familiar technological terms of today once had totally different meanings. This fun activity allows students to explore those old definitions.

199. Once It Was…

Objective: To determine old or archaic meanings of today's tech terms.

- *With your partner, you are going to have fun finding out what some words we use every day used to mean.*
- *Technology has created its very own vocabulary, but some of the words used to belong to what we will call* old vocabulary. *For example, a* bit *is the smallest unit of measure on a computer, but in old vocabulary it means a small, indefinite amount or scrap.*
- *When I cue you to start, brainstorm and jot down as many technological words as you can. Keep brainstorming until I cue you to stop.*
- Cue to start. Allow about five minutes before cueing to stop. By then students should have 10 to 20 words. If students are stuck, you might brainstorm words as a class, then have partnerships choose specific words for which to write old and new vocabulary.
- *Now examine your words and try to figure out if any of them belong to old vocabulary. If they do, what did they used to mean? They probably still mean that today, even if we use them mostly with technology.*
- *Not all the words might have belonged to old vocabulary. But if you think a word did, write its old definition beside its technological definition.*
- *If you don't know the old vocabulary definition, make it up.*
- Cue to start. Stop whenever you want to change focus.

* * *

Sample Tech Terms with Previous Meanings

address	surfing	virus	tablet	flaming
cloud	spam	worm	thumbnail	frozen
anchor	411	browser	application	hit
android	86	hardware	blob	host
apple	bookmark	java	boot	server
cookies	endpoint	platform	bug	programmer
hot spot	firewall	desktop	burn	
navigate	hacker	twitter	crop	
thread	ram	tweet	excel	

Stress Attack

Most of these techniques have been borrowed from therapeutic disciplines, such as acupressure, reflexology, meditation, mindfulness, stretching, fitness, wellness, and emotional freedom technique.

The activities in this section not only are quick and easy, but also offer life skills, little gems that students (or teachers) can take away and use in their daily lives when stress, anxiety, frustration, boredom, and even anger get in the way of positive behavior. These motivators can all be done independently; there is no need for teacher direction once they have been practiced once. Even if students don't actually believe they get any great sense of calm or release from them, at the very least they will get a few minutes of positive distraction.

As an adult, consider this: you are stuck in traffic; waiting far too long in a doctor's office; in a heated argument or uncomfortable meeting; standing in line anywhere. Heat builds; tension mounts. Why not make a Stress Attack? Trust me. They work!

As for students: every day they face myriad experiences in which they feel threatened, anxious, nervous, frightened, lonely, unsure, or just plain annoyed. If you introduce these activities in class, perhaps one or two of them will be remembered and used effectively to defuse negative situations. All it takes is for you to point out that any one of these snappy activities can, and indeed *should*, be used in daily life. A good idea would be to talk about when, where, and how this might happen. An even better idea: use them often to refocus your class!

While Stress Attack refocusers are not connected to specific subjects or content areas, they are listed in the chart on pages 19–22 under Life Skills.

- These activities use only brains and bodies: no props (except for Chew Two on page 152), no outside incentives, no competitions.
- They are not connected to curriculum. They can be carried out quickly and easily, and can be incorporated into any class, any subject, any time, with any age group.
- They quickly relax and energize, and can be done anywhere, at any time.

Tips for using Stress Attack:
- It is appropriate to quickly discuss the effects of each activity after its use—or not, depending on time, place, and students' needs.
- Share with students the thought that everything they do right here, right now, is a gift to their future selves.
- If you are feeling stress from an unfocused and disruptive class, chances are that your students are experiencing stress too. So these stress-relieving quickies work on many levels.
- A good idea would be to invite students to list their favorite stress attackers and enter them on a tablet, notepad, or social media, if they feel comfortable documenting them. This makes them more likely to reuse them when needed. Or perhaps students can start a blog describing their favorite stress-attacking activity and invite others to write reactions.

We all know that our minds are constantly in a state of being busy. We worry, we overthink, we plan, we predict, we categorize, we wonder, and we catastrophize all the time, even (this means students *and* teachers) in class. Diana Winston, a director at the UCLA Mindful Awareness Research Centre states, "The more we practice coming back to the present, the less anxious we will feel." Stress Attack refocusers encourage mind focus, even for just a few moments. They help the brain stop running and slow down briefly, which, in turn, helps the rest of the body calm down and become more grounded.

200. Forced Smile

Objective: The act of smiling, even if it's an artificial, forced smile, creates a change in the autonomic nervous system that produces feelings of well-being.

- *Sit or stand tall.*
- *Consciously tighten all your facial muscles, especially in your forehead and jaw.* This is where tension is held. The jaw can be tightened by forcefully jutting it forward and grimacing.
- *Hold for a silent count of 15.*
- *Now relax your face.*
- *Tighten your shoulders and upper back by hunching and holding for 15 seconds.*
- *Now relax your shoulders. Consciously let them go.*
- *Tighten and hold the lower half of your body for 15 seconds. Squeeze everything.*
- *Now relax your entire body and force a huge smile.*
- *Hold the smile for 15 seconds.*

Note: 55% of people yawn within five minutes of seeing someone else yawn, so getting the whole class to yawn shouldn't be too tough.

201. Fake Yawn

Objective: Studies have suggested that yawning temporarily increases the heart rate (like a shot of adrenalin) and also cools the brain.

- *Sit or stand tall and pull your shoulders back to completely open your breathing airway.*
- *Take a big breath and let it out slowly.*
- *Try to force a huge yawn.*
- *Attempt several until you achieve the perfect fake yawn. I'll tell you when to stop trying.*
- Watch for success or lack of success and judge the time accordingly. Usually 60–90 seconds are enough.
- You can take this quickie to a competitive level by finding the biggest yawn in the class.

202. Loud Silence

Objective: This activity involves complete inactivity, focusing on awareness of silence.

- *Sit very comfortably with both feet on the floor. Slouching is allowed this time, as comfort is key.*
- *Now open your inner ears and listen carefully to everything, but being completely silent yourself.*
- *Try to focus on the silence. What sorts of background noises can you hear?*
- *Think only of the silence.*
- *How does the silence make your ears and head feel?*
- Maintain for at least 60 seconds.

Debrief: Silence can be very loud. This quickie begs for follow-up discussion.

Note: For use only in a safe environment: i.e., not driving, walking, or moving at all.

203. Flip It in Color

Objective: Associating a color with a texture often helps students to visualize the color as well as better experience body changes.

- *Please sit down comfortably.*
- *Close your eyes and imagine a bright, shiny, red screen in front of your closed eyes.*
- *Form in your mind a single sentence describing the current negative situation you are in. For example, "I am distracted and restless."* Identify the common problem and form this initial clarification sentence for the class.
- *Now flip the color you are seeing behind your closed eyes to deep blue or soft black, like a cushiony, dark, velvet cloth floating in front of your eyes.*
- *Now flip the initial problem identification statement into the opposite statement: "I am paying attention and calm."*
- *Repeat this sentence over and over in your mind as you look deeply at the cushiony, deep color.* Pause for about 30 seconds to allow this visualization.
- *Now visualize your whole body. How does it feel now?*
- *Keep repeating the positive statement and seeing the dark color until I call you back.* Wait for up to two minutes before cueing to stop.

204. Lung Bellows

Objective: Deep breathing, for up to ten repetitions, improves lung function, helps reduce stress, and heightens the relaxation response—a quick dose of breath-based oxygen therapy.

- *Sit or stand very tall with your shoulders back to open your breathing airway.*
- *Move both arms into the goalpost position.* Demonstrate and practice this: upper arms parallel to the floor, forearms bent up at 90 degrees so that they look like goal posts.
- *Now pump your arms in and out in front of you, firmly and rhythmically.*
- *Let's practice one together. You breathe in when arms are back and your chest is spread; you breathe out as your arms move in so that elbows and forearms are touching.* The arms become bellows pumping the lungs.
- *We will do ten repetitions together.* Count slowly about 15 seconds for each inhale and 15 for each exhale.

205. The Effort/Achievement Connection

Objective: To help connect awareness of how hard students work with their accomplishments.

- *Sit comfortably and focus on the current situation that is causing you (us) a problem. We'll call this the* negative situation.
- *Create a mental sentence describing the situation: for example, "I hate this class and I'm terrible at it."* You can formulate this statement for students if necessary. *Say it over in your mind.*
- *Now consciously make a connection between effort and achievement, related specifically to the negative situation: for example, "If I pay attention, the work will be easier."* You can create this statement for students. *We will call this the* positive alternative.
- *Note that the positive alternative requires effort in order to be achieved.*
- *Until I cue you to stop, in your mind continue to connect the negative situation and the effort you need to make to achieve the positive alternative. In other words, put the two statements together and say them over and over: "I hate this class and am terrible at it, but if I sit up and give it some effort I will eventually get the work."*
- *You can think of different positive alternatives if you want to, or keep focusing on the first one.* Watch for restlessness and stop the activity after no more than two minutes.

Optional Debrief: Have students quickly jot down an effort–achievement connection they can recall.

Notes:
- It's a good idea to demonstrate this tapping technique before asking students to use it. Taps should be firm but not painful.
- This activity comes from Emotional Freedom Technique, an established psychological method.

206. Tap Technique

Objective: Tapping releases negative energy and promotes a feeling of well-being.

- *Sit/stand with your eyes open/closed.* Teacher's choice—I prefer sitting with eyes closed.
- *Using the first two fingers of your dominant hand, tap quickly and repeatedly between your eyebrows.* Allow 20 seconds, then cue to stop.
- *Now using the first three fingers of both hands, tap quickly and repeatedly on the bones just beneath your eyes and toward the outside corners of your eyes.* Allow 20 seconds, then cue to stop.
- *Now we will repeat both sets of tapping again until I say stop.* Allow for at least three sets, more if desired.

207. Ear Yoga

Objective: Studies have shown that ear manipulations like these can help you disconnect for a few moments and return to the moment feeling calmer and more energized.

- *Sit/stand calmly and close your eyes.* Teacher's discretion—it might not be feasible to do this eyes closed; for example, if the group is outside.
- *Using your thumbs and first fingers, firmly rub, pull, and pinch the entire outside of both of your ears.*
- *Move from the lobes to the tops and back down again. If you have piercings, rub gently around and over them.*
- *Continue until I cue you to stop.* Allow about 60 seconds.
- *Now gently cup both ears with your palms, as if you are holding a seashell over your ears, to block out sound and air flow.*
- *Now sit with your ears cupped and listen.* Or *Now make gentle circles with your hands in one direction, then the other, for about 30 seconds.*

Notes:
- The pressure applied during pinches and pulls should be firm but not painful.
- This entire sequence should be done by the teacher as the students are doing it.

208. Finger Focus

Objective: This reflexology-based technique has been shown to reduce anxiety, release helpful endorphins into the system, and generally encourage a feeling of well-being.

- *Sit calmly and comfortably.* Standing works too.
- *Think of your hands: how amazing they are: how important they are.*
- *Keep your focus completely on the hands.*
- *Now pinch every fingertip between the thumb and first finger of the opposite hand.* Demonstrate how to press up and down on the nail.
- *Next pinch each fingertip sideways, pressing the sides of each nail inward.* Demonstrate.
- *Next pull each finger firmly away from the palm, then rub it up and down briskly five or six times.*
- *Now gently pinch the webbing between your fingers. As you pull off the webbing between two fingers, let those fingers slide together.*
- *Now massage the soft spot between thumb and first finger by rubbing in a circular motion for about 20 repetitions. Repeat on your other hand.*
- *Finish with a brisk shake, as if shaking water from hands.*

209. Focus Fix

Objective: Visualization enhances concentration, reduces anxiety, and has even been known to reduce headaches.

- *Quickly scan the room/gym/field until you find a focal point, either a real point in your surroundings—like a light, a picture on the wall, a door—or an imaginary focal point in your mind.* The latter is more difficult and might not work as well with younger students. If an imaginary focal point is chosen, remind students they must "see" it with their eyes open.
- *Sit/stand comfortably and stare at your chosen point. Do not allow your vision to leave this point until I cue you to stop staring at it.*
- *Think only about the focal point. Look closely at it. Concentrate on the tiniest details and try to memorize them.* Allow 60 seconds. Give the Stop cue.
- *Now close your eyes and "see" the focal point in your mind. Look in your mind at all the details.*

Notes:
- This is one of the better stress attackers for calming chatty brains and helping them return to the present. Sometimes our heads are too full, too fast-speed-ahead, to be productive.
- It is a good idea to use a real focal point the first time this activity is used, then move on to internal, imaginary focal points if desired. Good imaginary focal points include a flame, a rainbow, a flower.

210. Toe Wiggles

Objective: Toe wiggling (a form of reflexology) relaxes the entire body. Because the feet are meridians that master the body, toe wiggling alternates between stimulating and relaxing the whole body and facilitates free-flowing energy.

- This can be done sitting, standing, or lying down.
- *Think about your feet, in particular your toes.*
- *Inside your shoes, wiggle the toes of both feet up and down vigorously 10 to 12 times. Count silently to yourself.*
- *Now rest the toes while you silently count to five. During this rest period, pay attention on the warm tingly feeling in your toes.*
- Repeat the sequence twice or until you give the Stop cue.

211. Chew Too

Props: Pieces of mint-flavored gum

Notes:
- Cortisol is a steroid hormone released in response to stress that has negative effects on the body.
- The small inconvenience of having to collect the chewed gum is well worth the benefits of this activity.

Objective: Chewing gum has been shown to beat stress, lower anxiety, and reduce cortisol levels.

- *I am going to give each of you a piece of gum. Unwrap it and put it in your mouth.*
- *When I give the Start cue, chew the gum as hard as you can.*
- *Chew vigorously until I cue you to stop. Then immediately stop chewing. Take the gum out of your mouth and wrap it in the paper it came in.*
- *During the chewing, I want you to concentrate on what your mouth, cheeks, and tongue feel like.*
- *Pay attention to the flavor and texture of the gum.*
- Give the Start cue and allow chewing for two minutes.

Note: It's hard to worry or feel anxiety when counting backward, even in your mind. Why do you think medical staff ask patients to count backward while they are waiting for anesthesia to kick in?

212. Back Up

Objective: To quiet the brain.

- *Sit or stand comfortably. If possible, close your eyes.*
- *Silently, in your head, start counting backward from 100. For younger children, it can be from 20 or 10.*
- *If you get to 0 before I tell you to stop, do it again.*
- Allow one or two minutes, depending on age of students.

213. Face It

Objective: These reflexology techniques help calm the mind and draw energy to the head, while providing a positive distraction.

- *Stand or sit comfortably, with your eyes open/shut* (depending on circumstances).
- *Put the first two fingers of each hand on your temples.* Demonstrate.
- *Gently massage in a circular motion for 20 circles, then switch directions for 20 circles.* Do this with them so you will know when to cue the next step.
- *Now use the first three fingers of each hand. Starting in the middle of the forehead just above the eyebrows, gently massage in small circles moving toward the hairline, then back again. The direction of circles doesn't matter.*
- *Now, on your own, repeat both actions two or three times until I cue you to stop.* Allow no more than 60 seconds.
- *Next, using one knuckle, press firmly under the nose on the midline of upper lip. Hold light pressure there until I tell you to stop.* Allow 20 seconds.

214. Stand Tall

Notes:
- The difference between towering and cowering is inner posture. It has nothing to do with height.
- The ability to physically hold a position is a reflection of mental hold. It is a reflection of strength, structure, and confidence.

Objective: Standing as tall as possible increases inner confidence and reduces stress.

- *Keep your feet flat on the floor about hip-width apart.*
- *Adjust your weight so it is evenly distributed over the entire soles of your feet.*
- *Take a big breath and stretch your spine taller and straighter as you exhale.*
- *Keep trying to get taller with each exhale for about 10 repetitions.*
- *Now breathe normally and experience the feeling of being as tall and straight as a tree or a tower.*
- *Pay attention to the feeling of your chest being open, of your shoulders being back and down, and of your back being very firm.*

Notes:
- Studies have shown that tension is carried in the inner elbows and behind the knees, where tightness goes unnoticed. As a result, the arms and legs eventually do not straighten completely, leading to shortened muscles and ligaments and, in turn, to other problems.
- This is not a race. The idea is to consistently reach upward rhythmically, higher and higher.

215. Sky Reaching

Objective: To stretch the inner elbow tendons that tend to shorten and tighten when you are experiencing stress.

- *Sit or stand very tall, breathing normally.*
- *Alternating arms, reach high above your head, as if attempting to touch the sky with your fingertips.*
- *Make the reaches directly over your head, not off to the side.*
- *Keep reaching and trying to make each reach higher than the one before. Be sure to completely straighten each arm at the elbow.*
- *But be careful—don't go on your toes* (if standing) *or raise your butt off the chair* (if sitting).
- *Keep reaching until I cue you to stop.* Allow at least 60 seconds.

Note: Caution students against hyperextending their knees by using their hands to push down on the knees when legs are straight. This is not ever a good idea. They can straighten their legs as much as they can without using their hands.

216. Wall Pushing

Objective: To release energy by imagining you are pushing it away, while getting the benefit of a simple stretch.

- *Sit sideways in your desk or facing front on your chair. Be sure you have room to stretch your legs out in front.*
- *When I cue you to start, straighten one leg then the other straight out in front of you. Push with your legs as if pushing against a wall.*
- *Try to imagine you are pushing away something that is bothering you—a little annoyance, a small fear, or a minor problem.*
- *Keep your feet flexed. Try to push with your heels while pulling your toes up toward the fronts of your legs.*
- *When extended, your legs should be parallel to the floor or approximately level with the chair seat, and your knees should be as flat as possible.*
- *Do this slowly. Follow my counts.* Count slowly, 2–4 seconds per push.
- Continue for about 60 seconds or until you notice fatigue in your students. It doesn't take long if they are really trying to extend and push.

217. Chest Opening

Objective: This stretching activity promotes flexibility and deep breathing, both of which have a calming effect. It helps the body relax.

- *Open your chest very wide by stretching your arms out and down.* Demonstrate holding your arms at about a 45-degree angle from your body.
- *Pull your shoulders back and point your fingers toward the floor. Your palms should be facing forward.*
- *Now take a big breath in and hold it until I tell you to exhale.* Have them hold for as long as possible, at least five seconds.
- While they are holding, tell them what will happen next. *When you exhale, you will reach forward as if rounding your body over a huge beachball with just your fingertips touching. Do that now.*
- *Don't breathe while stretched over. You will breathe in when I cue you to start all over again.* Cue to repeat the sequence after about 5 seconds.
- *Remember to reach out and down as far as you can on the inhale, and curl your back around and out over the "beachball" when you exhale.*
- Repeat the sequence 10 times.

Index

ideas & inspiration

FROM EXCEPTIONAL TEACHERS

No More "I'm Done!"
Fostering Independent Writers in the Primary Grades
Jennifer Jacobson

No More "I'm Done!" demonstrates how to create a more productive, engaging, and rewarding writing workshop that helps nurture independent, self-directed writers. Jennifer Jacobson guides teachers from creating a supportive classroom environment through establishing effective routines, shows how to set up a writing workshop, and provides an entire year of developmentally appropriate mini-lessons.

2010 | Grades K–2 | 176 pp/paper | RA-0784 | $19.00

The Construction Zone
Building Scaffolds for Readers and Writers
Terry Thompson
Foreword by Donalyn Miller

In *The Construction Zone,* Terry Thompson identifies four critical processes to deepen your understanding and improve your practice of instructional scaffolding to better support students as they build independence. Thompson encourages teachers to enhance their use of the traditional gradual release process through five actionable steps—show, share, support, sustain, and survey—and in doing so provides procedures and techniques to help them establish and maintain strong scaffolds throughout the instructional day.

2015 | Grades K–4 | 216 pp/paper | RA-0869 | $22.00

Reading Power
Adrienne Gear

Reading Power promotes reading comprehension with a wealth of effective strategies that help students think as they read. Using both nonfiction and fiction texts, Adrienne Gear shows teachers how to get students to zoom in, question and infer, find the main idea, and make connections to create meaning from the written page.

2015 | Grades K–8 | 144 pp/paper | RA-8310 | $24.00

Did you know...
you can receive Stenhouse's e-newsletter for FREE?

"It is one of the e-mails I make a point to read from top to bottom. There is always something that I use in teaching my classes. Thanks for making my job much easier and more effective."

—Georganna Ahlfors, Instructor, Los Angeles, CA

Stenhouse
PUBLISHERS

Professional Resources by Teachers for Teachers

www.stenhouse.com | 800.988.9812

ideas & inspiration

FROM EXCEPTIONAL TEACHERS

100 Minutes
Making Every Minute Count in the Literacy Block
Lisa Donohue

A comprehensive look at literacy and learning, *100 Minutes* shows teachers how to fit balanced literacy into a daily 100-minute literacy block using a framework of whole-class instruction and writing sessions, combined with independent work. It also offers strategies for dealing with the important elements of literacy instruction, including sharing and conferencing, using exemplars, creating success criteria, providing effective feedback, and thinking critically and analytically about all kinds of texts.

2012 | Grades K–6 | 160 pp/paper | RA-8276 | $22.00

Classroom Routines for Real Learning
Daily Management Exercises That Empower and Engage Students
Jennifer Harper and Kathryn O'Brien

Classroom routines are the well-oiled machines that make a classroom function. Routines can also provide the groundwork for a learning environment that nourishes student-driven learning. Whether they're used to start the school day or build classroom community, routines can help maximize learning by providing stability, consistency, and time management skills for teachers and students.

2015 | Grades K–6 | 128 pp/paper | RA-8297 | $24.00

Catching Readers Before They Fall
Supporting Readers Who Struggle, K–4
Pat Johnson and Katie Keier

Every teacher of reading plays a vital role in helping to catch those readers for whom learning to read does not come easily. Through examples from both adults and children, the authors explain the complex network of strategies that proficient readers use—strategies that struggling readers have to learn in order to construct their own reading processes. This book contains a wealth of resources and a free study guide online.

2010 | Grades K–4 | 288 pp/paper | RA-0781 | $24.00

Stenhouse
PUBLISHERS
Professional Resources by Teachers for Teachers

www.stenhouse.com | 800.988.9812

Sign up to receive *Newslinks* at stenhouse.com/newsletter

"I look forward to receiving your online newsletter, and find in every issue information I can share with my elementary school staff."
—Margaret Crowley, Principal, West Allis, WI

"Stenhouse Newslinks is my favorite newsletter. I get so much useful information about education from it."
—Carol Burken, Middle School Teacher, Cedar Rapids, IA